AF574884

Gold's Rounds

Footprints Series
Jane Errington, Editor

The life stories of individual women and men who were participants in interesting events help nuance larger historical narratives, at times reinforcing those narratives, at other times contradicting them. The Footprints series introduces extraordinary Canadians, past and present, who have led fascinating and important lives at home and throughout the world.

The series includes primarily original manuscripts but may consider the English-language translation of works that have already appeared in another language. The editor of the series welcomes inquiries from authors. If you are in the process of completing a manuscript that you think might fit into the series, please contact her, care of McGill-Queen's University Press, 1010 Sherbrooke Street West, Suite 1720, Montreal, QC, H3A 2R7.

8 *Doctor to the North*
Thirty Years Treating Heart Disease among the Inuit
John H. Burgess

9 *Dal and Rice*
Wendy M. Davis

10 *In the Eye of the Wind*
A Travel Memoir of Prewar Japan
Ron Baenninger and Martin Baenninger

11 *I'm from Bouctouche, Me*
Roots Matter
Donald J. Savoie

12 *Alice Street*
A Memoir
Richard Valeriote

13 *Crises and Compassion*
From Russia to the Golden Gate
John M. Letiche

14 *In the Eye of the China Storm*
A Life Between East and West
Paul T.K. Lin with Eileen Chen Lin

15 *Georges and Pauline Vanier*
Portrait of a Couple
Mary Frances Coady

16 *Blitzkrieg and Jitterbugs*
College Life in Wartime, 1939–1942
Elizabeth Hillman Waterston

17 *Harrison McCain*
Single-Minded Purpose
Donald J. Savoie

18 *Discovering Confederation*
A Canadian's Story
Janet Ajzenstat

19 *Expect Miracles*
Recollections of a Lucky Life
David M. Culver with Alan Freeman

20 *Building Bridges*
Victor C. Goldbloom

21 *Call Me Giambattista*
A Personal and Political Journey
John Ciaccia

22 *Smitten by Giraffe*
My Life as a Citizen Scientist
Anne Innis Dagg

23 *The Oil Has Not Run Dry*
The Story of My Theological Pathway
Gregory Baum

24 *My Peerless Story*
It Starts with the Collar
Alvin Cramer Segal

25 *Wrestling with Life*
From Hungary to Auschwitz to Montreal
George Reinitz with Richard King

26 *Never Rest on Your Ores*
Building a Mining Company, One Stone at a Time
Norman B. Keevil

27 *The Making of a Museum*
Judith Nasby

28 *Gold's Rounds*
Medicine, McGill, and Growing Up Jewish in Montreal
Phil Gold

Gold's Rounds

Medicine, McGill, and Growing Up Jewish in Montreal

Phil Gold

McGill-Queen's University Press
Montreal & Kingston • London • Chicago

ISBN 978-0-2280-1758-5 (cloth)
ISBN 978-0-2280-1847-6 (ePDF)

Legal deposit second quarter 2023
Bibliothèque nationale du Québec

Printed in Canada on acid-free paper

This book has been published with the help of a grant from the Montreal General Hospital Foundation.

We acknowledge the support of the Canada Council for the Arts.
Nous remercions le Conseil des arts du Canada de son soutien.

Library and Archives Canada Cataloguing in Publication

Title: Gold's rounds : medicine, McGill, and growing up Jewish in Montreal / Phil Gold.
Names: Gold, Phil, author.
Series: Footprints series (Montréal, Quebec) ; 28.
Description: Series statement: Footprints series ; 28 | Includes bibliographical references.
Identifiers: Canadiana (print) 20220488266 | Canadiana (ebook) 20220488355 | ISBN 9780228017585 (cloth) | ISBN 9780228018476 (ePDF)
Subjects: LCSH: Gold, Phil. | LCSH: Physicians—Québec (Province)—Montréal—Biography. | LCSH: Jewish physicians—Québec (Province)—Montréal—Biography. | LCSH: Montréal (Québec)—Biography. | LCGFT: Autobiographies.
Classification: LCC R464.G585 A3 2023 | DDC 610.92—dc23

To Evelyn:
My debt to you is immeasurable,
as is my love.

Contents

POEM

To Evelyn

On the Occasion of Our 60th Wedding Anniversary

We've had six wonderful decades
of happiness, love, and accolades.
Evelyn, you've always made our family work,
you have that really marvellous quirk
for Ian, Josie, and Joel, and then
all the grandkids who've followed them.
2020 has been a rather strange year
but still, we've had our days of cheer,
and although we would sometimes groan
we've learned that we're never alone.
We have, indeed, a wonderful prize:
children, and grandchildren, of every size.
Last fall I finally got my head together
and went back to work in early winter weather.
Whatever the day was like, I always knew
that I would soon come home to you.
But then it happened, lightning quick:
we were swallowed up by the pandemic.
That rotten little virus, with all its might,
started killing people left and right.
My protective colleagues told me, very true,
"We don't want you in the ICU."
They sent me home to avoid any strife.
They sent me home to my very dear wife.
We've spent these hundreds of days
in pretty similar groundhog ways.
Whatever the future days may send
I'll always be here with my very best friend.

The Golds in 2006. From left: Joel, Natalie, Adam (in arms), Alex (Django), Ian, Evelyn, Phil, Benji, Zack, Josie, Matthew (baby), Cleve, Michael.

Preface

This book is written primarily for my children and grandchildren. Along with my wife, Evelyn, you have made my life worthwhile. Each of you holds a key to my happiness and every hug is a joy. I hope this memoir is the beginning of a family history that carries on for ages to come.

The recollections that follow are simply that—recollections. Many things lost to memory remain undescribed, and may have been as important as what remains. In addition, what I remember happening has acquired the patina of time (for better or worse) and is coloured by the observer, me.

Evelyn—"Bubbie" to our grandchildren—has often chided me for not writing down these memories sooner. Perhaps I procrastinated to avoid dredging up some of the things I've known, all along, would have to be included. My younger son Joel, a brilliant psychiatrist, may be better suited than I am to understand how my early years as a child of immigrants moulded my adult life as a husband, father, and now grandfather. Those formative experiences around Saint Lawrence Boulevard may also help explain my choice of work, hobbies, and avoidance of other things.

Growing up on what is now called the Plateau, I always feared getting lost. Not just lost in place—I have a poor sense of direction—but also lost in time and person. It remains a strange feeling. I've never been entirely sure of who I am or how I got to be here.

My life feels somewhat like a short wander: south on Saint Urbain Street, from Bancroft Elementary to Baron Byng High School, then across Jeanne Mance Park to McGill University. Then another short wander across campus, from Physiology to Medicine—and up the hill to the Montreal General, the home of my career for so many years. Were these meanderings really decisions I made consciously? Or did they simply happen?

Perhaps in this memoir I'll find out.

From the vantage point of 2022, everything in my life seems to have gotten better with time. A recurrent thought remains that I haven't done enough... and yet, with these few words, I've made a start. Perhaps this memoir will be therapeutic for me and others.

Life, to my parents, was about adapting to change. Talking to my mother as an adult, I understood that perspective more clearly. She felt fortunate. She had escaped the lethal antisemitism of her native land and wasn't chattel to anyone. Life went on. She had more choices and independence now than she ever dreamed possible. How could she be anything but lucky?

As I was writing *Gold's Rounds*, my working title was "Fortunome," a word I made up to capture my sense of the third great pillar that all our lives rest upon: luck. Our *genome* comes from our parents; our environment or *epigenome* shapes the expression of who we are; but without a good *fortunome*, life's odds turn against us. This book is my attempt to express how lucky I have been throughout my life. I had inspiring teachers, good health, opportunities to work, new scientific horizons to explore, and most of all a wife I have loved dearly for over sixty years. When it comes to luck, my cup runneth over. If you could sit on a cloud before being born, and were given a choice between good genes, good environment, or good luck, for me there's no contest. Always take luck.

So, without further ado, here is a taste of my world and I how I came to be here.

Gold's Rounds

Phil Gold, aged four or five, wearing a formal outfit, circa 1940.

PART I

Growing Up on the Main

The Story of My Parents

To start, my name is Phil Gold, not Philip (growing up, we couldn't afford the "ip"). I was born September 17, 1936, at the Royal Victoria Hospital in Montreal, a first-generation Canadian child of two Polish immigrants.

My mother, Rose (Raizel) Spindler (December 24, 1917–April 14, 2004), was from the town of Ozarow (Ojerov in Yiddish). She and her four siblings came over with their mother probably in 1931–32. Her father, Pinchus Spindler, a shoemaker, had crossed the Atlantic in the late 1920s and with the help of his brother Benny sent back money for the family to follow. My mother's entire extended family left Poland in dribs and drabs over the 1920s and '30s, all of them emigrating to Montreal thanks to my financially successful great-uncle Benny.

My mother's family left Poland, of course, to escape the antisemitism and pogroms (campaigns of terror and killing) that were a fact of life for European Jews. As an illustration of this, when my mother was a teenager walking home from school one day, a man on a horse rode up and whipped her incessantly. She staggered home, her legs bloody and swollen. The rider gave no explanation. She was a Jew: that was reason enough.

My father, Yankel Goldmitz (December 17, 1913–March 11, 1990), anglicized to Jack Gold, was born and raised in Opatow (Apt in Yiddish), about twenty kilometres away from my mother's hometown. The two met for the first time in Montreal at a Jewish community event, courted, and got married at the Beth Yehudah Shul at 210 Duluth Street East, on December 17, 1935. He turned twenty-two the day of their wedding, and she was one week shy of eighteen. I came along exactly nine months later.

My father had emigrated to Canada on his own as a teenager, around 1930, all too happy to leave behind the small-minded constraints of the shtetl. He

The main market in Ozarow, Poland, in September 1939, the month the Nazis invaded.

was a freethinker, especially in matters of religion and politics, and his heartfelt beliefs were based on the teachings of Karl Marx. He had apprenticed as a tailor while still in Poland and was very good at his work. After emigrating, he became a sewing-machine operator in the sweatshops of Montreal's garment, or schmatte, industry. I remember as a boy hearing my father's fellow workers say he was the best tailor they had ever seen. Later on, he would start his own short-lived garment business before becoming a superb designer of women's clothes. But back in the early 1930s, in the years after he arrived, any money he didn't require for the necessities of life got sent back to Poland. The plan, of course, was for his family members to follow him to Canada.

But that is not what happened. My paternal grandfather was apparently intent on becoming a vintner and purchased a vineyard near Opatow sometime in the 1930s. Perhaps the money he used was his own, perhaps it included the funds my father sent back to book his family passage on a steamer.

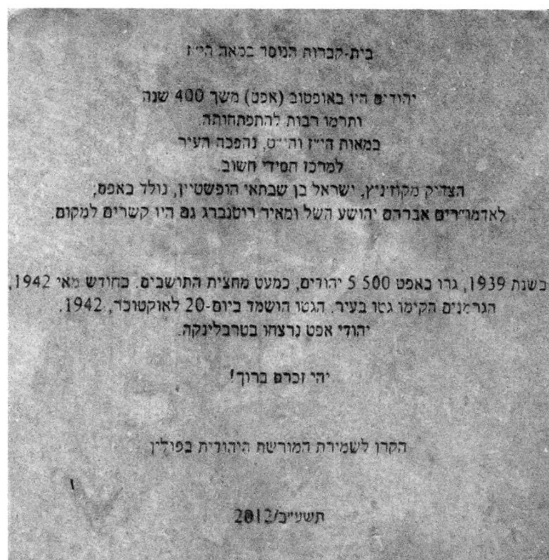

RIGHT: Postcard from Shloime Birnbaum of Montreal to his father Chil in Ozarow, returned unread, dated September 11, 1939.

LEFT: Memorial plaque, Opatow. "Jews have been in Opatow (Apt) for 400 years and have contributed greatly to its development. In the 17th and 19th centuries, the city became an important Hasidic centre. The Tzaddik from Kuznitz, Israel Ben Shabtai Hofstein, was born in Apt. Hasidic spiritual leaders Avraham Yehoshua Heschel and Meir Rotenberg also had connections to the place. In 1939, 5,500 Jews lived in Apt – nearly half of its residents. In May 1942, the Germans established a ghetto in the city. The ghetto was demolished on October 20, 1942. The Jews of Apt were murdered in Treblinka. May their memory be blessed! The Foundation for the Preservation of Jewish Heritage in Poland 2012/5772."

On September 1, 1939, the Nazis launched their blitzkrieg attack, triggering the start of World War II, and overran Poland in barely a month. If the Goldmitz clan had any inkling of what was about to happen, it was too late to get out. As in every Jewish community in Poland, the Nazis forced the Jews of Opatow and Ozarow into ghettos—first open, then closed—where they were summarily shot, starved, worked to death, or herded onto trains bound for the Treblinka and Auschwitz death camps. Insofar as I am aware, my father's entire family, which was apparently extensive, was murdered along with the rest of their community in the ghetto or the death camp.

I was six years old in 1942 when my father's letters to family in Opatow started to go unanswered. I remember asking him why they didn't write back.

"They can't," he said. "They must be in detention."

For the next two years, my father, like so many Jews outside Europe, probably chose to see the chaos of war as the reason for the silence rather than believe the swirling rumours that something terrible had happened. But in late 1945, as survivors began to trickle out of Europe, we learned the unspeakable truth. Whenever someone visited us to share more terrible news, I was told to leave the room. My father never spoke about his family again.

"Just tell me about them," I would plead with him in the years that followed. "Did I have uncles or aunts? Do you have any photos?"

But asking such questions was forbidden. All they did was cause my father greater distress and push him deeper into his shell. He remained traumatized by survivor's guilt for the rest of his life. In later years, still wanting to know

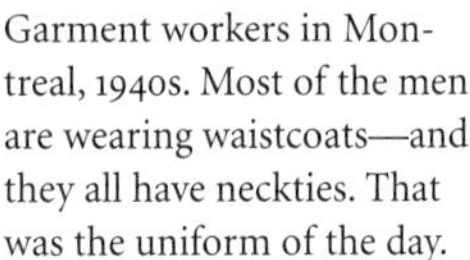

Garment workers in Montreal, 1940s. Most of the men are wearing waistcoats—and they all have neckties. That was the uniform of the day.

something—anything—about my forebears, I tried an indirect approach and bought dictation machines for him, on two separate occasions, so he could tell the story of his family privately for posterity. The tapes remain unused to this day. When my father died in 1990, the memory of his family turned to ashes.

I am, indirectly, a survivor of the Holocaust.

As if he hadn't suffered enough, my idealistic father was dealt a second tremendous blow after the war when he lost his political beliefs. As a young man he believed in Communism, but reports emerging from Stalin's Russia after the war revealed the ideology to be a vicious and murderous hoax and his faith unfounded.

I shared my father's left-wing ideals when I was very young, carrying picket signs at garment-worker strikes that he helped to organize. But around 1948, when I was twelve, I began to form my own opinions and our political arguments started. We would argue in persistent and increasingly heated fashion for many years to come. And despite a certain rapprochement as adults—I would hear from his friends that he was proud of my medical career—the pattern of our relationship was set. Such patterns are hard to change.

Me with my parents Yankel Goldmitz (anglicized to Jack Gold) and Raizel (Rose) Spindler, Montreal, around 1940.

But regardless of our differences, I admired my father greatly. I cannot fathom the courage of my parents and relatives, crossing the ocean almost a century ago to arrive in an unknown land that most definitely did not flow with milk and honey. Until they learned one or more foreign languages, my parents had few prospects, almost no money, and no means by which they could make their way in the wider world.

I have often asked myself: were I in their position, would I have had the guts to pick up roots and do what they did? I sincerely doubt it.

But maybe, as the saying goes, *When you ain't got nothin', you ain't got nothin' to lose.*

Living on the Main

Shortly after I was born, my parents moved out of my grandmother's flat on Duluth Street and rented a third-floor apartment at 4543 Saint Lawrence Boulevard, just north of Mount Royal Avenue. As Stephen Leacock put it, I decided to go with them.

Saint Lawrence Boulevard (or St-Laurent, as it is written in French) was commonly called the Main because it was the main street running north from the old heart of the city, with cross-street addresses beginning at 1 East and 1 West on either side. The Main also symbolically divided the island's two main cultural groups: the French, or francophone, majority in the east and the English, or anglophone, minority in the west. Clustered in the middle were Jewish immigrants like us, our households rising along its length like doughy braids of challah.

In 1937, when we moved in, my parents paid $27 per month, and for the next seventeen years that amount never changed. Nowadays in the stylish and expensive Plateau, illegal rent increases and "renovictions" are common. But like most building owners at the time, our landlord, Monsieur Jean, never raised the rent.

Our flat was small, comprised of a kitchen, a double living room–parlour, and a bedroom. Next to the radiator in the kitchen was a child's little green table and matching green chair, where I sometimes ate my meals, and in the parlour a cot behind a curtain, where I slept. The apartment's one bedroom, my parents' room, had no door, so any intimacy would have to have occurred after I fell asleep. When my younger sister, Malk, came along in 1945, she slept in my parents' room for a few years before moving to another curtained cot on the other side of the parlour.

My parents liked each other, but they also argued a lot. One of my earliest memories is of sitting in my little green chair, very still, hoping that if I remained completely quiet—sort of disappeared—they would stop. I found their arguing fearful. My mother was certainly no pushover—she gave as good as she got—but my father could be scary. I have no doubt that my aversion to direct confrontation with loved ones today arises from such episodes.

My father left early in the morning to go to the sweatshops before I got up for school, and he came home around 6 p.m. After supper he went to "the club" for a few hours of pinochle and other card games with his friends, returning home after I'd gone to bed. When I heard his footsteps coming up the stairwell, I would get a queasy feeling and think, *He's back.*

OPPOSITE: *Young boys in the road* by Paul-Marc Auger, taken in the Plateau neighbourhood around 1940.

ABOVE: St. Lawrence Boulevard, looking north, near the old Warshaw Supermarket, August 1944. On the left is L. Berson and Sons Monuments, with its stone-lifting apparatus. The sign for Schwartz's Delicatessen can be seen top right. In the distance is the Vineberg garment factory at the corner of Duluth (renamed the Berman Building in 1951). The decorative post in the foreground is a telephone box for police use only.

Vintage ad for Kodak's Brownie Camera. When Solly departed, he left me his Brownie. The whole episode is still a painful memory.

My mother, in contrast, was always home. From breakfast, waving goodbye from the window as I left for school, to welcoming me home in the afternoon, she brought me up virtually alone. She was warm and nurturing, if a bit possessive, and we seldom disagreed. Our days were pleasantly routine.

My parents were proud to be Jewish, and my mother kept a traditional kosher home, more or less, but my father's strong political beliefs meant that any sense of religious Judaism had to be acquired outside the home. But between my grandmother's stories in Yiddish, blue-collar antisemitism on the street, the Morris Winchevsky Jewish afternoon school, and my own dawning sense of the Holocaust, I figured out pretty quickly what it meant to be Jewish.

Babbeh's Place

When I was a toddler, my mother would walk me over to my grandmother's home. By the time I was seven or eight, she trusted me to get there on my own. "Okay, go carefully," she would say and wave to me from the window as I left. Some days I would play with friends on Clark Street or just wander around the neighbourhood on my own. But my favourite place to end up was always my grandmother's. As the saying goes, I slept at home, but I lived at Babbeh's place.

Babbeh—Pesa Tobah Spindler—lived at 4053 de Bullion in the third-floor apartment on the northeast corner of Duluth Street. Technically, it was my aunt Helen and uncle Dave Kaplansky's place, but everyone called it Babbeh's place. Many Jewish immigrants lived along de Bullion back then. The street had previously been called Cadieux, and in the 1920s was a red-light district

Uncle Solly holding Lily and me, summer 1938 or 1939, near Babbeh's place at 4053 de Bullion.

so notorious that Mae West's Broadway play *Sex* opened in a brothel there. Cadieux was renamed de Bullion in 1927 and "cleaned up" during the venereal disease scares of the 1930s and '40s, creating opportunities for immigrants to move in.

Babbeh's husband, Pinchus, my grandfather, had been a shoemaker who came to Canada alone in the late 1920s under the sponsorship of his brother Benny, a quiet man with a nasal voice. Babbeh and her children (including my mother) followed him in the early 1930s, crossing the Atlantic by steamer with more financial support from Benny. In Montreal, my mother attended grade school and helped her father in his shoe shop but, sadly, a year or two after the family's arrival, Pinchus died suddenly on his way home from the synagogue. He was found lying in the snowy street in the winter of 1933 or 1934. I never knew my grandfather Pinchus. By Jewish tradition, since I was named for him, he had died prior to my birth. Babbeh later told me that he had fallen and "frozen to death." As a doctor, I would guess that it's more likely he had a heart attack, collapsed, and died quickly. But whatever the reason, Babbeh was left a widow with few resources, no trade, and no English

or French. Thankfully her older children were already in their twenties and working, and happy to look after her.

Babbeh and Pinchus had five children: Hymie, Helen, Sam, Rose (Raizel, my mother), and Solly (Saul). Hymie, the eldest, lived a few streets over on Hotel de Ville (we called it City Hall back then) and had left a divorced wife and a child back in Poland to start a new life in Canada. I can only imagine the pain that caused, and their likely fate in Poland. Uncle Sam—a sweet man built like a tank—also lived nearby. Aunt Helen and her husband, Dave Kaplansky, made a home for Babbeh with them on de Bullion, and Uncle Solly also lived in the large apartment. Helen and Dave's daughters, Lily and Goldie, were my best friends and constant childhood companions. All of the men in the family worked in the schmatte trade. Most of them had started in it back in Poland, and they had little choice in their new environment but to continue.

OPPOSITE: The Spindlers in Montreal, circa 1933. From back left: Dave Kaplansky, Helen, Babbeh Pesa, and Zaidie Pinchus, my namesake. Seated: Rose, Solly, Sam. Hymie (not pictured) had not yet arrived in Canada.

Uncle Solly and I were the best of pals, despite our difference in age. He taught me how to throw and catch a baseball and took me to Delorimier Downs from 1946 into the early 1950s to see Jackie Robinson and other baseball greats play for the Montreal Royals. Solly also had a knack for making toys from wooden cut-outs with a handsaw. He and uncle Dave were like surrogate fathers to me. Solly married somewhat later in life, and out of the faith. I'm certain this didn't pose a problem for most of the family—we weren't very religious—but it was probably a source of deep concern for him because soon after he married, he cut off contact with his siblings and disappeared completely from our lives. Before he left, he must have told my grandmother what he was doing because after he was gone, she gave me his Brownie camera, saying Solly wanted me to have it. It's still a painful memory today. I often tried to find Solly in the ensuing years, as did Lily and Goldie, but without success.

On Saturday evenings, my parents would leave me at Babbeh's place with Lily and Goldie, and we would listen to Montreal Canadiens games on the radio. Babbeh loved hockey and screamed her lungs out listening to Foster Hewitt. Her favourite players were "Morris Rish-ei" (Maurice Richard) and "John Belliball" (Jean Béliveau). She never did get name pronunciations right, but who cared? Well into my twenties, I believed the gall bladder was located behind the right ear, as she would frequently rub that area and exclaim, "*Ooyy, de gall bladdeh.*" I had to relearn human anatomy in medical school.

Alongside the radio in the living room sat a large phonograph, which took 78 rpm records. One of Babbeh's favourite songs was "Bésame Mucho" played by Xavier Cugat. Solly taught Lily, Goldie, and me how to dance to that number and others. Even now, when I hear that song, I am flooded with memories.

Babbeh spoke Yiddish exclusively, and as a result Lily, Goldie, and I grew up speaking fluent Yiddish as well. She would occasionally throw the odd

RIGHT: *Cugat's Favorite Rhumbas*, and *Cugat Cavalcade*, Canadian editions of the LP that Babbeh loved to play.

English word into her sentences and clearly she understood enough to enjoy the hockey games over the radio—but when Helen and Dave got a rotary telephone installed in the kitchen, Babbeh didn't trust the new device, referring to it disparagingly as *di shreklikhe zakh* ("the terrifying thing"). Disembodied voices of strangers seemed to spook her. The fact that the voices were speaking English or French probably didn't help. But whatever the reason, for many years she refused to come to the phone.

In 1948, Solly accompanied Babbeh to the Montreal courthouse to take her Oath of Citizenship. After the judge gave a short speech about what it meant to be a Canadian citizen (words I suspect Babbeh did not fully understand), he proceeded to the swearing-in ceremony:

"Repeat after me," said the judge. "I solemnly swear…"

To which Babbeh replied, "I and Solly swear…"

No one seemed to mind.

Babbeh was a good citizen and a great role model. She was loving, had a strong personality, and created a warm household in which her grandchildren could thrive. She helped us understand who we were and where we came from. I've tried to take these qualities with me throughout my life.

At the end of a day at Babbeh's place, when it was time for me to go home, she would send me back to my mother with a chocolate bar in my pocket and a two-dollar bill (a princely sum back then) hidden inside the wrapper.

Babbeh passed away on December 14, 1966, at the Jewish General Hospital in Montreal, surrounded by her loved ones. She was eighty-two years old. I think of her often, especially when I ask my children or grandchildren for help with computer programs and fondly remember her difficulty with the telephone.

TOP: Delorimier Downs, 1933.

MIDDLE: Jackie Robinson shaking the hand of teammate George "Shotgun" Shuba after scoring a home run in the Montreal Royals' season opener in New Jersey on April 18, 1946. Newspapers across the continent carried this iconic photo. For the Royals' first home game in Montreal on May 1, a wild crowd of 15,745 fans (second largest in stadium history) packed in to see their new rookie star and future Hall of Famer.

BOTTOM: "Morris Rish-ei" and "John Belliball" in spring 1958, holding the third of five consecutive Stanley Cups. Doctors at the Montreal General Hospital would give players on the Canadiens a physical before the season got underway, under the leadership of Doug Kinnear and later David Mulder. I examined Jean Béliveau once in the late 1960s. It was the easiest physical I ever gave. He was in great shape.

Babbeh (Pesa Tobah Spindler) around 1960, outside a summer rental cottage in Val Morin or Val David. She was illiterate, having had virtually no schooling in Poland, but she was very intelligent, and like a lot of people, she distrusted new technology. When my aunt and uncle got a rotary telephone installed at their home, Babbeh refused to speak to the disembodied voices on di shreklikhe zakh ("the terrifying thing").

A Story from the Old Country

Sometimes Babbeh told stories of the old country in Yiddish to Lily, Goldie, and me.

When we were very young, these were children's stories. One involved a figure called "Bubkaleh Bear," a mischievous bear-like creature who ran around the forest near Ozarow, getting in and out of trouble. Bubkaleh Bear was always successful with his tricks and always avoided punishment. It's no coincidence that Babbeh didn't believe in punishing children either.

As we grew older, Babbeh's stories grew more realistic in ways that reflected the harsh treatment of Jews in Poland.

One was the chilling tale of my mother being whipped by the man on horseback.

Another story involved the Polish postman who delivered mail irregularly to the shtetl. When he had a letter from "Amerikeh" addressed to my mother's family, the postman would wave it in the air in front of them but not give it to them. A few weeks later, when he would finally deliver it, the envelope was often open and any enclosed money gone. Antisemitism takes on all kinds of forms.

Lily and Philly and Goldie

My first two real friends were my cousins Lilian Kaplansky and her sister, Goldie, who lived with their parents, Helen and Dave Kaplansky, at Babbeh's place on de Bullion Street. For fifteen years I saw them almost daily. But I never called her Lilian, and she never called me Phil. It was always Lily and Philly and Goldie.

Whenever I showed up at the door, some sort of food was already prepared that I had to eat *immediately*. Only then could I go out and play in the street. Sitting across the kitchen table from Lily and Goldie, I truly believed that all girls had runny noses when they ate hot soup.

As the eldest cousin, Lily was owed a certain respect—regardless of our not-infrequent arguments—while Goldie, a couple of years younger than me, was the quiet tagalong in our troika (a role that changed quickly as we grew). We made snowballs in the winter and played at hopscotch, tag, and stickball the rest of the year, always pausing for the odd car to roll by. Sometimes we used a skipping rope to tie up Goldie or one of her friends to a lamppost or fire hydrant. Just for fun, of course! But whatever the make-believe game, Lily was always there to protect us. On one occasion when some kids from the block started hassling Goldie and me, Lily drew up her four-foot, six-inch frame, stuck out a knuckle, and said "You wanna fight them, you're gonna have to fight me first." To my amazement, they left.

As my university career became more and more time-consuming, I saw Lily and Goldie less often. Some years we met only during Jewish holidays, at bar mitzvahs, or at weddings, but the distance of time never changed anything. We always had great fun catching up on family events, and Lily took genuine pride in my medical career. Whenever we talked, I was filled with her warmth and reminded of our lifelong friendship.

Lily went to Teachers College, became a fine teacher, and married David Zacharin, who had started a dental practice. They had two children, Noah and Laura. Goldie went into administration and worked at the office of a Jewish day school in Montreal. I've often heard people say that Goldie ran the place. She married Hershey Warshawsky, an outstanding histologist and colleague of mine at McGill University, who developed an international reputation for his work in the structure and renewal of tooth enamel. Goldie and Hershey have three children: Paul, Bryna, and Avrum.

Sometime in the late 2000s, Lily apparently started to develop symptoms of dementia. I became aware of this in 2010 when I needed some vintage family photos for my induction into the Canadian Medical Hall of Fame, many taken by Uncle Solly, of our days growing up on the Plateau. As family historian, Lily kept all such things. She went through her collection with great care and came up with a terrific selection for me. But after I told her that the hospital photographer would need to hold on to them for a week, to make high-resolution copies, she became distressed and called me every

LEFT: Lily and Philly with Goldie as a baby, early 1940s.

RIGHT: Me and my cousins, again, mid-1940s. Both pictures were taken in the Laurentians.

few hours to ask when I would be returning her photos. After about twenty calls I realized something was amiss, got the photographer to change his schedule, and returned the photos in two days, to her immense relief. But this wasn't the Lily I knew. I discussed the situation briefly with David, her husband, who was, obviously, aware of the matter.

I stayed abreast of Lily's condition, and a few years later, Goldie called me to say Lily had been admitted to the Jewish General Hospital. She had become violent at home and David could no longer deal with it. She was then taken to a seniors' residence, without much in the way of diagnosis, a fact about which Goldie was unhappy. Lily was probably suffering from dementia, but had she had a proper evaluation, and was she getting the best possible care? Goldie was a great sister, standing up for Lily the same way Lily had stood up for us in those early years. Soon after, however, Lily showed further evidence of violence, tearing up bedclothes and causing a general commotion, which required her admission to the Geriatric Unit of the Jewish General Hospital.

The first time I visited Lily there, I found her at a bridge table in the common area with her head resting on the table. I scratched her back and she looked up.

Evelyn Gold, *Past, Present & Future*, a portrait of my childhood with Lily and Goldie growing up on the Plateau. Babbeh's place was on the third floor of the orange building in the foreground, with windows looking out onto both streets, de Bullion and Duluth, above the corner store.

"Philly," she said.

Oh, thank G-d, I thought, *she knows who I am.*

But that was the last word she ever said to me.

We walked around the ward holding hands like we did as children. I talked about the old days at Babbeh's place. But Lily could only manage curt responses like "I'm tired" and "I want to go home." After a while I asked if she needed anything. She declined all offers. I returned her to her room, we kissed goodbye, and I promised to return.

I was glad I'd taken a cab to the hospital that day because I wasn't able to concentrate after my visit. I kept having flashes of our lives as kids: playing, dancing, walking around the old neighbourhood, arguing, dinners at Babbeh's place, the faces of other kids on the block. Our greatest concern back then was which game to play next.

On another occasion, Goldie, Hershey, Evelyn, and I went to visit Lily. She was quite comfortable with the other three, but it soon became obvious that I frightened her, so to save her further distress, I left the residence and waited outside for the others. What had happened to the mind of my best friend and protector? Perhaps my son Joel, a psychiatrist with a brilliant

Chip truck, 1940s. "It's the aged oil."

understanding of the causes of mental illness, will discover some answers in the years to come.

Lilian Florence Kaplansky Zacharin died on February 15, 2019, at the age of eighty-four. Her family was by her side.

They Came by Horse and Buggy

When I was a child during the war, the street in front of Babbeh's house was frequented by men who came by horse and buggy. These were travelling salesmen offering their wares.

The first was the Chip Man, who sold small bags of french-fried potato chips for a nickel and nothing else. The chips were deep-fried in a vat of oil mounted on the cart. The oil may have been changed once a year, at most, and people regularly explained the chips' wonderful flavour was due to the "aged oil." Much like fine red wine. The Chip Man never lacked for customers.

The next to pass was the Ice-Cream Man. You could have any flavour you wanted as long as it was vanilla. I can still conjure up the taste of that ice cream. Few things have ever tasted better.

Occasionally the Knife Sharpener would pass, slowly ringing his bell, then waiting for the housewives to bring out their knives. He'd pull his wagon halfway onto the sidewalk, start the grindstone spinning with his foot, and hone anything that needed sharpening: knives, tailoring scissors, can openers, axes for chopping wood. A fascinating profusion of sparks would fly from the stone where it met a blade, and the sharpened metal would gleam like new.

LEFT: Horse-drawn milk cart outside the Elmhurst Dairy (now Parmalat) on St. Jacques Street, Montreal West, 1942.

ABOVE: Dairy products from Elmhurst, including "Major Treat" ice cream, butter, and a Lift-N-Pull milk-bottle cap.

The Milkman passed by every day early in the morning, selling all forms of dairy out of his wagon: eggs, sweet or salted butter, cottage cheese, cooking and table cream, buttermilk and regular milk. The milkman knew by memory each household's usual needs, but if you had special requests, you marked them on the milkman's little order sheet and left it in an empty milk bottle outside your door. I heard the milkman not only at Babbeh's place but out the window of our flat on the Main. As he passed below with his horse, *clip-clop clip-clop* would echo up the street in his wake. Before going to school, I brought our order upstairs from the doorstep.

The Fruit Man passed twice weekly and sold apples, pears, and other fruits grown locally in season. Grapes, bananas, and other fruit grown faraway started to arrive after the war. Housewives would come out to the Fruit Man's buggy, squeeze and assess the wares of the day, buy or decline.

Then there was the Ice Man, his buggy loaded with one- and two-foot blocks of ice cut from the Saint Lawrence River the previous winter. The Ice Man had a distinctive cry, *aye-EEE-isss*, which drew the housewives out to the street. "Single or double?" he'd ask, sweeping back a rubber sheet to reveal layers of sawdust and wood chips on top of the ice, which kept it cool. He'd pick up a block with ice tongs—a spiked metal tool that resembled huge pliers—and schlepp it up flights of inner and outer stairs, dripping all the way, and deposit it directly into the kitchen icebox. The brute strength of the Ice Man delivering a fifty-pound block of ice each day always amazed me.

The Coal Men, who delivered coal to the house every two weeks, frightened me. They would swing a heavy chute from the wagon, open a metal grate near the sidewalk, and funnel coal into the hole, where it tumbled

TOP: Home ice delivery.

BOTTOM: Prices of the City Ice Company on Craig Street (Rue St-Antoine).

ABOVE RIGHT: Horses hauling away ice cut from the St. Lawrence River, circa 1870. The recently completed Victoria Bridge, once called the "eighth wonder of the world," is in the background

into the basement furnace rooms of houses and apartment blocks. The coal men were always covered in black dust: clothes, hats, hands, faces and necks, and the apparition of those faces burned into my childhood memory. I could never discern their expression behind the dust. To my shame, it made me imagine that they were evil men, but the sadder truth is that the coal dust, over time, likely caused them severe lung disease.

Like horse droppings washed away by rainwater, the world of the horse and buggy is long gone. But memories remain.

Bancroft School

I did not go to kindergarten. As a result, I entered grade one at Bancroft Public School in September 1942. My schooling, in one form or another, has never really stopped.

Bancroft Elementary was on Saint Urbain Street—two blocks from my home on Saint Lawrence Boulevard—and the fastest route there was via the alley facing our front door. This took me directly to a large door at the south end of the school. But I couldn't enter through that door. That was the Girls' Entrance. Even though our classes were co-ed, I still had to use the Boys' Entrance at the other end of the building.

Those first weeks of school, my mother bought me milkshakes and school supplies at the Bancroft Stationary Store and Snack Bar, which had just been purchased by Hymie and Freda Sckolnick. Hymie and Freda turned it into one of the best places to eat on the Plateau, and locals started referring to the snack bar as "Beauty's," which was Hymie's bowling nick-

Bancroft Elementary School on St. Urbain Street today, with a view of the former girls'-side entrance.

name (whenever he threw a strike or a good spare, people would shout "Beauty!"). Beauty's is now, literally, a world-famous diner, in particular for the "mish-mash," an omelette made with hot dog, salami, green pepper, and fried onion, and home fries on the side. But it's still located on the corner of Saint Urbain and Mount Royal, still a family-run business, and still my favourite breakfast stop whenever I'm in the old neighbourhood. Hymie continued to work in the restaurant until shortly before his death. Often, when Evelyn and I took our grandchildren for breakfast there, Hymie was wont to say, "I know you. You're famous. Are you a doctor or a lawyer?" So much for neighbourhood fame!

For the first half of grade one, my mother paid 25¢/week to our downstairs neighbour, Danny Taran, who was a few grades ahead of me at Bancroft, to make sure I got to school without going astray. Danny went into the schmatte business and real estate after that, but his first business deal was with my mother! After a few months, I walked down the alley to school by myself. The buildings facing the alley were cold-water flats, the cheapest available. For the next half-dozen years, it never struck me as odd that people lived facing the lane, in conditions far worse than my own. Our place on the Main always had heat, hot water, and food on the table. Apparently, not so in the lane.

My first teacher was Miss (not Ms.) Esther Hoffman. Miss Hoffman always wore a grey smock and carried a white handkerchief tucked inside her right sleeve, which she occasionally pulled out to delicately dab her nose or wipe chalk dust away from her eyes. To a six-year-old in 1942, that white handkerchief was the height of propriety and chic.

Miss Hoffman could be stern, but she was also loving, compassionate, and a wonderful teacher. At a time when very few immigrants could afford record players, she brought her own to the classroom and charmed us with Prokofiev's symphony for children, *Peter and the Wolf*. The narrator, Basil Rathbone, named each instrument as it entered the score and explained which character it represented in the story. This was my first real introduction to music.

Miss Hoffman loved books, and the entire back of our classroom, wall-to-wall along the back shelf, was devoted to storybooks. Almost all children's books at the time were printed in black and white (coloured inks were reserved for the war effort), but somehow Miss Hoffman's books had incredible, full-colour illustrations. Once we had learned to read, she would let us take one book home for the weekend. I trace my lifelong love of books back to that experience.

Miss Hoffman also read out loud to us. As my friend Mort Levy remembers, *Lassie Come-Home* was the most popular novel for children in the 1940s, and just like the Harry Potter series today, the demand for it was insatiable. The Bancroft library held a single, prized copy—with a one-year waiting list to read it. Practical as ever, Miss Hoffman brought her own copy to class and read *Lassie* out loud to everyone.

Miss Hoffman also read us poetry, including Robert Browning. Yes, Robert Browning for six-year-olds! The opening lines of his poem "Rabbi Ben Ezra" have stayed with me ever since:

Grow old along with me!
The best is yet to be

OPPOSITE PAGE: Boys in Ms. Liefer's grade five class at Bancroft. I'm standing in the back, second from left, wearing suspenders.

TOP LEFT: The Bancroft Snack Bar (aka Beauty's), early 1950s.

TOP RIGHT: Album cover for Prokofiev's *Peter and the Wolf*, narrated by Basil Rathbone and conducted by Leopold Stokowski, 1941.

Years later, when I began teaching medical students at McGill, I thought back to Miss Hoffman's class and grasped her secret: she made students *want* to learn. She was aware that "telling stories" and using metaphors was a much better way to teach than by reciting facts. A teacher can only teach students, not "learn" them. Learning is the student's part of the contract. That philosophy has served me well for sixty years.

Esther Hoffman and I maintained a happy connection. She followed my career with pride. When Evelyn and I were married, Miss Hoffman turned up at our wedding ceremony, unexpectedly. She kissed me on the cheek as we exited the chapel and wished us good luck.

Some decades later, when she began to feel very sick, Miss Hoffman came alone to the Emergency Room of the Montreal General Hospital.

"Call Dr. Phil Gold, he was my student," she said.

I came right down to Emergency. It was clear she was having heart problems. I had her admitted to the ward on which I was working, where I could see her every day. It was a privilege to give something back to her, after so many years, but also distressing to learn that this wonderful woman had no one else to help her during such times.

One morning during my rounds, she asked me if I remembered Browning's fine words about growing old and "the best is yet to be." I assured her I'd never forgotten them. She smiled.

"Browning got it wrong," she said. "Growing old sucks!"

She passed away a few weeks later.

The original Hairy Potter: Eric Knight's 1940 classic *Lassie Come-Home*, made into a movie in 1943.

LEFT: L'chaim, Mort!

RIGHT: Mort Levy and yours truly at Bancroft School for its hundredth-anniversary celebration, February 2017. Mort and I met at Bancroft on our first day of school in 1942, and have been best friends ever since.

I am forever grateful to Esther Hoffman—a great teacher and an important person in my life.

Meeting Mort

On my first day of school at Bancroft in 1942, I made a friend.

"Hi, I'm Phil," I said. "What's your name?"

"Mort."

Mortimer Levy was a quiet young man. So quiet, in fact, there were times when the only way I knew he was alive was because I could hear him faintly breathing at the desk next to mine. But for whatever reason, we hit it off.

We've been the best of friends for almost eighty years.

Mort's family lived at 4650 Henri Julien, apartment 4, a few blocks farther from school than my place, and starting around grade three we got into the habit of walking to school together. Mort would ring the street-level bell, walk up two flights to our third-floor flat overlooking the Main, then stare silently at me as I finished my breakfast. On winter mornings, if it had been snowing, the snow on his boots would melt on the kitchen floor as he waited, driving my mother crazy.

Then we'd walk to school.

"Whatcha do last night?" I'd ask.

"Nothing much."

"That math homework was pretty easy."

"Yeah, I did it while I was listening to the game."

When it got really cold, Mort's mother dressed him well enough for an expedition to the Antarctic, with a long scarf wrapped up to his eyes and a woollen toque covering his forehead and eyebrows. In the narrow slit between, you could just make out the person inside was Mort. If you knew him well.

"What do you plan to do for the rest for the day?" I'd ask him as we walked home from school.

"I'm not sure. I'll tell you tomorrow."

Like so many Jewish kids in the neighbourhood, Mort and I hung out at the YM-YWHA on Mount Royal, just across from Fletcher's Field (now Jeanne Mance Park). We played marbles, card games, street hockey, and just kidded around a lot. As we grew into adolescence, our pursuits expanded to touch football, movies, and girls. Mort and I always found people-watching an entertaining pastime.

At the end of high school, both of us went to McGill. We studied honours physiology together, went to medical school together, and taught at the same institution, McGill, for the rest of our careers. I worked and did research at the Montreal General Hospital while Mort became a nephrologist at the Royal Victoria Hospital, doing his research in his lab in the Department of Physiology at the McIntyre Sciences Building.

When I got married, my best man was—who else?—Mort Levy.

And when Mort found Marsha, a terrific person, he became a "cosmopolitan man-about-town," often staying up past 10 p.m. Their family became bigger and more wonderful, later on, with the arrival of Brian and Josh, and their wives and children.

In all this time, Mort and I have never had a significant disagreement.

Malk, My Sister

For almost a decade growing up, I had no siblings. Then in spring 1945, as the Allies were declaring victory in Europe, my mother told me she was pregnant. Unexpected or not, my parents seemed quite pleased and, on August 24, 1945, along came a baby girl.

Listening to my parents discuss their traditional options, the baby could be named after a second or third cousin on my father's side, "Bobbeh" Malkah, but we had little or no relationship with these distant cousins, so I came up with the brilliant idea of calling the baby Queenie, since *malke* means "queen" in Yiddish. This was nixed immediately. I then suggested calling the baby Margie, which my parents liked. Eventually my sister made her own choice, asking us to call her Malk within the family. The result today is that she's Malk to me and my family; Queenie to my daughter Josie's husband, Cleve; and Margie to the rest of the world.

Malk and I were a pair of "only children," born nine years apart. As the older brother, I often played the role of babysitter. On one memorable occasion, I was at home with my sister when the unmistakable smell of smoke

Margie "Malk" Gold, my sister, late 1950s. Any humming drives her crazy.

Malk and David's wedding at Beth-El Synagogue in Town of Mount Royal, August 7, 1966. From left: Phil, Evelyn, Ian (age four), David Markus, Malk, and proud parents Jack and Rose Gold.

filled our apartment. I called the fire department and the dispatcher said a firetruck was already on its way. Immediately, sirens began to blare outside the window. My one thought was to wrap Malk in a blanket and get out of the building quickly. In the narrow stairwell, the smoke was stronger and my eyes stung badly, but we made it out. Neighbours gathered around us on the street. They told me that I had saved my sister's life, which was nonsense: the fire was in the adjacent building. A few hours later, whatever was burning nearby was extinguished and Malk, my parents, and I were back inside our home, none the worse for wear.

When Malk was thirteen, she had to write a composition for school about a great Canadian. I suggested Lester B. Pearson, who had just won the Nobel Peace Prize in 1957. Malk thought this was a good choice so she wrote about Pearson. The following week I saw her teacher's positive response, but with one sentence circled halfway down the first page: "For his actions during the Suez Crisis, Lester B. Nobel won the Pearson Prize." Well, close enough!

Because of our difference in age, Malk and I seemed at times to be part of two different families. When she was starting grade school, I was more than halfway through high school at Baron Byng and doing very well academically. By the time I was finishing at McGill, Malk was just starting high school. Unfortunately, my sister had to endure the all-too-common refrain

"Why can't you get the marks that Philly gets?" Malk grew sick of this comparison.

"*Philly Philly Philly* is all I hear," she would say. "I'm not Philly and he's not me." Brava!

When I heard my parents comparing us, I would ask them to stop—but I should have been more forceful about it. Malk, to her credit, has never held this against me, which says a lot about the kind of person she is.

Malk married David Markus at the Beth-El Synagogue in the Town of Mount Royal on August 7, 1966, and then taught elementary school in Notre-Dame-de-Grâce for two years. David started his career as an accountant, but with his obvious ability, he became the sales manager for a furniture manufacturer, which took him and Malk to Toronto, Chicago, Los Angeles, and back to Toronto over the coming decades. During some of those years, Malk worked at the Ontario Ministry of Citizenship and Immigration; at Temple Menorah in Redondo, California; and at Temple Sinai in Toronto. Everyone who meets Malk knows she is terrifically talented. Not only did she teach herself graphic design and run Temple Sinai's program of publications, she also taught herself enough about Judaism to run a synagogue office!

Malk and David have four sons. Steven is a biological scientist; and Michael, Jeffrey, and Andrew have all gone into the technical and animation aspects of show business in and around Los Angeles. In 2013, Malk and David retired to their "winter palace" in La Quinta, California, and their "summer palace" in the mountains of San Luis Obispo, California.

Malk always makes her feelings known. When our parents used to visit her and David in Toronto in the 1970s and '80s, they would stay in the basement bedroom, where my father's frequent humming would drive her bananas. She would hear him humming through the floor and shout down, "Quit it already!"

"Malk, let me hum for you," I sometimes say to her coyly.

"You can scream, you can yell, but you can't hum!" she replies.

I do love my sister.

Mr. Muir and the Library

In 1946, I entered grade five at Bancroft School. World War II had ended the year before and a jubilant feeling of victory filled the air. Although I was a relatively shy kid at heart, the sense right after the war that anything was possible may help to explain why I marched into the principal's office in early November.

Mr. Muir, the principal, was a rotund man with a bulbous red nose. He scared me a little, to be honest, but I got up the courage to ask him a simple question.

LEFT: Parade on Mount Royal Avenue, 1941.

RIGHT: *V-E Day* by Conrad Poirier. A spontaneous party erupts on Saint Catherine Street around Phillips Square on May 7, 1945, as Montrealers celebrate victory in Europe and the end of war. In the background are Birks Jewelers, a streetcar, and many Union Jacks.

"Mr. Muir, do I have to come to school?"

"Yes."

"Why?"

"It's the law. And there are people called truant officers who have a list of the kids who don't show up. They go out and find the missing kids. Then the kids and their parents get into trouble."

He let this sink in for a moment, then continued, "But tell me, Phil, why don't you want to come to school?"

"We're learning the same things this year that we did in grade four."

"Oh?"

"I'm not learning anything new."

Mr. Muir thought for a moment.

"Well, as long as you pass all your class tests and do reasonably well, you don't have to spend every minute in the classroom. If you get bored, you have my permission to go to the library instead."

What a leap of faith that man took on my behalf!

For the next three years, I split my days between the classroom and the school library. I read more poetry by the Brownings (both Robert and Elizabeth Barrett), books by Mark Twain (*Tom Sawyer* and *Huckleberry Finn*), and books about Shakespeare, Michelangelo, and Leonardo da Vinci, and on and on.

Those days amid the library's dark-wood floors and endless shelves of books changed me. I realized that the great artists and scientists in those books thought things and knew things that were not known to anyone before. Soon I developed my own desire to know something unique. That hope would not come to fruition for twenty years, but it started in the library at Bancroft Elementary.

The Morris Winchevsky Yiddish School

I did not attend a Hebrew day school. Not only would this have been unaffordable for my parents, it was unconscionable for my father, given his secular, socialist beliefs. But my parents did want me to learn the cultural and political aspects of Jewishness. And so Monday through Thursday afternoons, after school ended at Bancroft, and on Sunday mornings, I walked one block north to the Morris Winchevsky Yiddish School at 30 Villeneuve Street West and Clark Street.

Morris Winchevsky was a prominent Yiddish poet, newspaper editor, and socialist leader from the turn of the century, and the little afternoon school in his name was set up by the United Jewish People's Order (UJPO).

In the school program, children learned to speak and read Yiddish, which I already spoke quite fluently, and we were taught a version of Jewish history that skipped the stories of the Patriarchs Abraham, Isaac, and Jacob to focus on the longstanding oppression of Jews: the pogroms of Eastern Europe, exploitation of blue-collar Yiddish workers, and our expulsion from virtually every civilized country on earth.

These lessons were not just academic: on the way home, I would face the wrath of Canadian francophone kids toward people of my faith. After a fair amount of bleeding, I learned to fight back and became "friendly" with some of these kids. When I asked why they had harassed me, they said it was because I had killed Jesus Christ. When I denied I would ever have done such a thing, they said that's what the priest told them in church, so it had to be true. It was left at that, so many years ago. I had met blue-collar antisemitism and faced it down. The white-collar brand would come later.

At my Yiddish school program, we also talked about emigration, specifically restrictions on Jewish immigration even after Canadian and American diplomats knew the Holocaust was occurring. Many Canadians would not learn of this shameful fact until 1983, when historians Irving Abella and Harold Troper published *None Is Too Many: Canada and the Jews of Europe 1933–1948*. At the Morris Winchevsky School, however, we knew it from first-hand experience. As we sat in our little classroom in Montreal in the early 1940s, tens of thousands of Jews in Europe were being murdered every day, many of them relatives of Montreal Jews, including my father's entire family.

The Morris Winchevsky model of learning was driven by a pure Marxian vision: the Soviet Union was meant to be our salvation and Communism was the answer to all our historical woes. During my preteen years I believed this, which made my father happy, since these were his beliefs too. Indeed, by the time I was ten or twelve, I was carrying picket signs alongside my father at strikes of the International Ladies' Garment Workers' Union (ILGWU); singing paeans in Yiddish to Birobidzhan, a proposed Jewish

LEFT TO RIGHT: Label of the International Ladies' Garment Workers' Union, my father's union. ILGWU promotional poster, late 1930s. The Triangle Shirtwaist Factory fire, New York, March 25, 1911.

homeland in Siberia; and could recite details of the Triangle Shirtwaist Factory fire in New York, where 146 young Jewish and Italian women immigrants died in the 1911 disaster. A memorial to the victims was finally approved in 2019.

By 1948, reports out of Russia began to show the enormous cracks in the Communist system and deep antisemitism among the commissars. The State of Israel was also founded in 1948, a world-changing event that split families and nations down the middle. I was barely twelve at the time, but my father and I started having enormous arguments over the dinner table, my mother playing unwilling referee, which sometimes ended with him slapping me.

I kept going to the Yiddish after-school program, as much out of habit as anything else, but I disliked having the party line being laid down to us. And yet whenever I threatened to quit, I was promoted to the next grade. I guess they needed the meagre fee.

One day in the winter of 1950, when I was thirteen, I walked up to Villeneuve Street and found a large padlock on the door. A story in the local newspaper relates what happened:

> Centre Padlocked by Police, Literature Seized, Home Raided. *The Gazette*, January 28, 1950
>
> In a concerted drive against what they described as "Communist activity" throughout the province, provincial and city police anti-subversive squad members yesterday padlocked a "cultural organization" building for a period of one year and seized a considerable quantity of literature in raids on a Jewish school and a private home.

Headquarters of the former United Jewish People's Order at the corner of Esplanade and Laurier, with its backlit balcony for inspiring speeches to the masses. It reopened in 1951 as the Farband Labour Zionist Centre (shown here), a definite move to the right of centre.

The "padlock law" was applied at the United Jewish People's Order centre, a two-storey building situated at 5101 Esplanade Avenue, while other raids were effected at the Morris Winchevsky School at 30 Villeneuve Street West, and the home of Berel Silverberg, at 4853 Esplanade Avenue. The latter is secretary of the order.

"Our investigation revealed that for at least one year, the centre had been operated as the locale and general headquarters of lectures, soirees and secret meetings of Communists," [said a police spokesman]. … [The raid] had been ordered by Premier Maurice Duplessis himself in his capacity as attorney-general of the province. … Police said that in addition to the literature, documents and lists of names bearing those of people who were "sympathizers of communism" had been seized.

Thus began yet another episode in the history of Quebec's infamous Padlock Law.

I rejected Communism, but my support for the working man, learned so young from my father and at Morris Winchevsky, has stayed with me to this day. My father eventually accepted that the Soviet Union and Nazi Germany were two sides of the same coin, but the realization shattered his worldview and, along with his survivor's guilt, remained a major trauma for him throughout his life.

Nowadays when I see Bernie Sanders with his scrappy attitude, shouting at the television camera in his Brooklyn-Jewish accent, I see my father's face and remember our heated political arguments.

Quebec provincial police padlock the front door of UJPO headquarters, January 27, 1950.

Street Fighting and the YMHA

When I went to play in the street as a child, the first French words I learned were "maudit juif" ("damned Jew"). This was usually followed by a punch to the face and some blood. Even as a child I knew enough not to cry—that would have shown weakness, and I wasn't going to do that. After a while I got tired of bleeding and found that a pre-emptive strike frequently brought the situation to a rapid conclusion, and the ruffians even became civil.

The Young Men's Hebrew Association (YMHA) played a significant role in my life. Back then, it was located on Mount Royal Avenue between Jeanne Mance and Park Avenue, across the street from what was called Fletcher's Field (now Jeanne Mance Park). I joined the Y, for a minimal fee of $3 as I recall, to use the gym and the pool, to play and watch basketball games, and to take boxing and wrestling lessons to defend myself better on the street.

My first clear memory of the Y, when I was very young, was walking into the building one day rather bloodied. There were four or five older boys there who formed a little group. They asked what had happened. I said I would wash up, it wasn't important. They asked again, and so I told them I had been beaten up by some French-Canadian boys on the street. That group from the Y went out, with me in tow, found my tormenters, and delivered a terrible beating—to the point where I had to pull one of them off, shouting, "Stop, you're gonna kill him!" I learned that day there were people who had my back, and that it was my obligation to provide the same kind of support to others, both physically and otherwise.

The last time I hit anybody in anger was when I was about sixteen years old. A young man walked toward me on the street, clearly with ill intent, and I just reacted quickly. He fell back and hit his head against a pole. And he did not move. A voice in my head said, *Your life is over. You've just killed someone.* Thankfully, he did move. I helped him get up, dusted him off, and he just walked away. I have never hit anyone in anger since then.

The Y was a major focus of our social lives. In my early teens, it hosted "mixed" meetings between boys and girls, painfully slow evenings that over the years were rebranded as Club Socials, where boys learned how to ask girls out on dates. Some guys learned faster than others, but it all seemed to work out in the end.

A Dollar for the Day

In my early teens, on Thursdays, my mother would give me a dollar for the day. My parents didn't have a TV yet (not until 1954) and there were no movies-on-demand back then, so I would often go to Wilensky's Light Lunch, on Fairmount, order the special (salami, bologna, and mustard on a toasted bun), and rifle through the novels on the store's second-hand bookshelf. ("Gold, are you just looking or do you plan to buy?" owner Moe would ask me if I read a book too long).

LEFT: The YMHA (later also YWHA) on Mount Royal Avenue, facing Jeanne Mance Park, in 1936. It was built by tobacco magnate and philanthropist Sir Mortimer Davis.

RIGHT: Local boxer Sammy Jacobs of the YMHA, circa 1939–1940. Note the Star of David inside a maple leaf on his shorts. Sammy was the hero of the community. He was a tough Jew.

Model United Nations conference of the Monty-Ikes (named after Generals Montgomery and Eisenhower) at the YMHA, March 1951. I supported the entry of Red China into the UN. I'm in the middle, and Mort is bottom right, smiling. Standing behind me in the sweater vest is Maynard Shapiro, who became a great surgeon at the Jewish General, and the boy sitting middle-row left is Morris (Moishe) Cohen, whose father owned the butcher truck in which I learned to drive.

But as I got older, on Thursdays Mort and I would go to the movies.

From 1927 to 1961, the age of admission to movie theatres in Quebec was sixteen. This was due to the Laurier Palace Theatre fire of 1927, in which seventy-eight people died, many children among them. And so before we got to the magical age, Mort and I often had to attempt several theatres, including the Regent and the Rialto way up on Park Avenue, before finding a ticket seller who'd take our money and let us in.

One Thursday, after being turned down at several theatres, we finally got into the Royal, on the Main up near Beaubien, the bottom of the barrel of movie theatres. The elderly gentleman who sold us tickets then walked the aisles, selling drinks, popcorn, and ice cream. From my point of view, our goal was to maintain a low profile until the lights dimmed. Mort had a different perspective.

"Boy, oh, boy!" he said loudly, snapping his fingers. "Two popcorn."

Before I knew it, I'd leapt over the seats and moved two rows away.

After a few months, Mort and I got to know the woman selling tickets at the Belmont Theatre on Mount Royal, near Saint Lawrence, and admission became easier. It probably helped that Thursdays at the Belmont were slow.

A dollar stretched a long way in the 1950s. The first 25¢ went to the theatre ticket: that covered three consecutive pictures at the Belmont, which were often movies that had premiered in first-run theatres only a few weeks before. Popcorn and a drink—the Special of the Day—set us back another dime.

Emerging from the theatre some four hours later, it was dinnertime. Mort would go home for dinner. But once the Belmont became our regular, I would usually go to Feldman's Delicatessen, right across the street on Mount

LEFT: The Rialto, 5723 Park Avenue, still the best art-deco theatre in the city.

RIGHT: The Regent Theatre at 5117 Park in 1930, now a Renaud-Bray bookstore.

Royal, and order a takeout "hot combination smoked meat and stuffed chicken sandwich," a Coke, and a spicy sausage called a karnatzel. That set me back 55¢ and left a dime for a comic book, usually Superman or Captain Marvel, which I bought on the way home and read during dinner.

Nowadays, an afternoon like that would cost a great deal more. And my old comic books might be worth millions!

The Long Summer

Throughout my childhood, polio was a constant fear. North Americans by the tens of thousands developed the disease every summer, and a great many victims were children. Thousands died, and the survivors often had lifelong disabilities. Like the recent COVID-19 pandemic, it shaped society.

Because polio spreads by the oral-fecal route, cleanliness and hygiene were major factors in its spread or inhibition, with the result that it was more prevalent in less clean and more crowded neighbourhoods. Montreal experienced several particularly virulent summer epidemics in the late 1940s and early 1950s. Public pools were closed, children were quarantined, and when September arrived, the schools stayed closed. Families who had rented summer cottages stayed there, feeling quite appropriately that their children were safer away from the city and avoiding close contact with other children.

TOP: The village of Lesage in the Laurentians. Mr. Lesage's house is on the far right. Just outside the frame is the other half of his semi-detached house, where we stayed. Behind the church on the left is the little train station where we would wait for my father to arrive on Friday evenings.

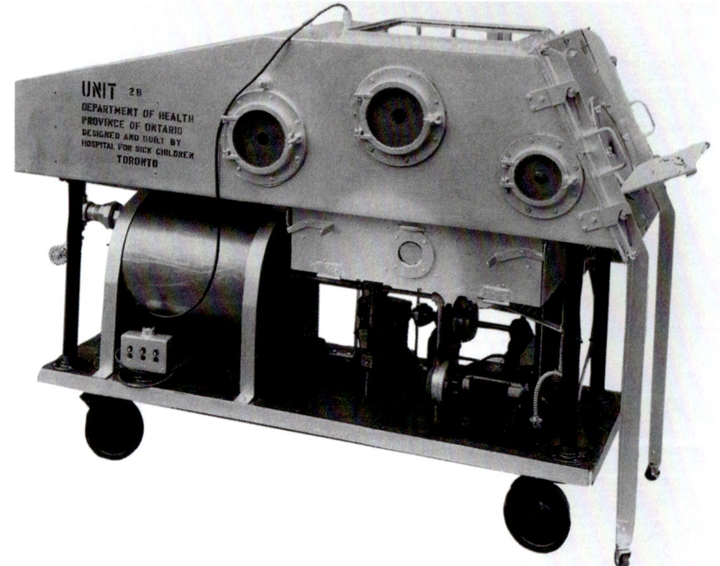

BOTTOM: A portable iron lung for polio victims, designed in the late 1930s by Toronto's Hospital for Sick Children.

For several years my family had rented a cottage in Lesage, a small village in the Laurentians just north of Saint-Jérôme. The landlord, Mr. Lesage, whose forebears had founded the village, was happy to let us remain there for as long as we thought necessary—at no further cost. As sometimes happens in life, we benefited from "the kindness of strangers," as Blanche DuBois famously says in *A Streetcar Named Desire*. But unlike Blanche DuBois, Mr. Lesage's offer to us was simple and sincere and came with no strings attached.

By the end of September, however, our summer supply of wood for the stove was running low. We gathered fallen branches from the surrounding forest to keep our uninsulated cottage warm in the chill fall nights. Then, one very cold night toward October, the temperature plunged quite dramatically. We lit the stove, but soon our wood supply was exhausted and the

Me in my favourite sailor's cap, with Malk, Lily, and Goldie in Lesage, circa 1952.

fire started to go out. The only option to avoid "the great chill" was to burn some of the furniture. Into the stove went a broken-up side table. In went the legs and rungs of a chair.

We made it through the night. The next day one of my parents visited Mr. Lesage and the matter must have been resolved—whether by payment (unlikely), replacement, or forgiveness—because we returned to the cottage in Lesage the next summer.

A few years later, when the Salk vaccine for polio appeared in 1955, it felt as close to a medical miracle as I've ever known.

Baron Byng High School

After seven years at Bancroft Elementary, Mort Levy and I walked two blocks south on Saint Urbain Street to the carved stone doorway of Baron Byng High School (BBHS). I was excited by the prospect of learning new things. Now, I was aware of the school's reputation for pranks and practical jokers, but I was still surprised on my first day to walk into my new homeroom, Room 37, and encounter a total lack of decorum. My fellow grade-eight students were trying to live up to the reputation of our new school. They jostled, pushed chairs into the aisles, threw paper balls around the class, and everyone was shouting. The reputation of BBHS was being tested.

After watching the mayhem for ten minutes or more, I realized our teacher would not, or could not, control it. So, I finally asked the two biggest guys I could find—future good friends Sam Borenstein and Morris Schwisberg—

RIGHT: Baron Byng High School. I remember Jack Waxman, nicknamed Kutter (cat in Yiddish), climbing up the outside of the building pretty much anywhere he wanted. Jack went on to open a candy shop in New York.

LEFT: Phil Gold, 1953, class president. My yearbook entry: Favourite philosopher: Aristotle. Favourite Quote: It's pre-t-t-y tough but that's the way it goes. Favourite Occupation: Arguing anything with anybody. Pet Aversion: People who borrow books — permanently. Ambition: Ph.D. Probable Destiny: Ph.G. (Phil Gold).

if they would like to be lieutenants. They weren't sure what that meant. I assured them they'd find out in a moment.

I climbed onto the teacher's desk and shouted for quiet. QUIET!

I declared that we had come here to learn, that we couldn't do this in a chaotic environment, and it was time to control ourselves. Then I declared myself Class President for Life and made it clear that anyone who had trouble with anything I'd just said should take it up with my lieutenants.

That seemed to do the trick.

Over the next four years at BBHS, we matured into young adults with good educations who could look after themselves intellectually, physically, and psychologically. Mort and I found a group of friends now, like us, older men and women, with whom we've kept in touch over the years. We were segregated in the classrooms—boys' and girls' classes were on entirely opposite sides of the school building—but happily there was always time after school and on the weekends for other activities.

The pranks never stopped—we were teenagers, after all—and one memorable event involved unscrewing all the desks in Row 5 from the floor and putting them in a closet. After recess, half a dozen students stood open-mouthed in the middle of the classroom, looking around, asking the teacher where they should sit. Hijinks like this were immortalized by Mordecai Richler in several novels at the fictional version of BBHS, which he called Fletcher's Field High School. Everything he wrote about Saint Urbain Street, Baron Byng, and the neighbourhood was more or less true. Mordecai was a terrific guy, some five years ahead of me at Baron Byng. Don't let anyone tell you he was a mean-spirited curmudgeon: like all Baron Byngers, Mordecai simply gave as good as he got.

In September 1949, when I entered high school, the Quebec school system was divided along religious, not linguistic, lines, with the somewhat absurd result that Jewish kids and other non-Catholic immigrants were considered Protestant for educational purposes, regardless of our actual religious affiliations. By the early 1920s, the rising enrolment of Jewish children in "Protestant" schools seems to have alarmed the board. Baron Byng High School, named after Canada's twelfth Governor General, was built effectively to ghettoize Jewish students, that is, to educate them while keeping them in their presumed place on the sidelines of society.

But quite the opposite happened. Instead of staying in "their place," Baron Byngers started showing up every spring on the list of top graduating students in the province. Jews are known as the people of the book for a reason: Jewish parents would rather go hungry than deprive their children of an education. The school turned out poets, artists, jurists, politicians, and professionals of every stripe—hardworking young citizens who would go on to fame locally, nationally, and internationally.

Even a partial list of successful Baron Byngers is impressive:

Harry Blank, seven-term Liberal MNA
Morris Fish, Supreme Court Justice
Alan Gold, Chief Justice of Quebec
Yoine Goldstein, lawyer, academic, senator
Harold Greenberg, film producer
A. M. Klein, poet
Irving Layton, poet
Sylvia Lefkovitz, painter and sculptor
David Lewis, Rhodes scholar, politician, leader of the NDP
Marilyn Lightstone, actress
Frederick Lowy, president of Concordia University
Rudolph Marcus, chemist, Nobel Prize in Chemistry
Herbert Marx, Quebec Minister of Justice and Superior Court Justice
Louis Nirenberg, mathematician, Abel Prize
Jack Rabinovitch, founder of the Giller Prize
Mordecai Richler, author
Fred Rose, Communist MP
Reuben Ship, playwright and screenwriter

Saul Levine, psychiatrist
Lionel Tiger, anthropologist
Sid Stevens, co-founder of Sun Youth

What was it about Baron Byng that produced so many remarkable people? For me, it was the chemistry of the neighbourhood, our shared circumstance as children of immigrants—and the absolute certainty that if we wanted more out of life than our parents had, it would not be given to us: we would have to go after it ourselves. The result was a hard-working, self-reliant, supportive environment in which young people thrived.

For Jewish kids back then, our entire lives were contained within ten long blocks from Van Horne down to Pine Avenue and the five blocks from Park Avenue across to Saint Lawrence. Everything you needed was more or less within that stretched-out rectangle. Every store you passed belonged to somebody's father, whom you probably knew—Beauty's restaurant, Putter's Delicatessen, Gann's butter and cheese, Segal's grocery, Schreter's clothes. And if you didn't have the money that week to buy groceries, you could get it on credit until you did. You knew everybody and everyone knew you, and everybody and everything was "just down the street." Kids didn't have to belong to teams or schedule games: you just showed up at Fletcher's Field and played ball with those around, or you went off to explore on the Mountain. And the Jewish religious holidays Rosh Hashanah (the New Year) and Yom Kippur (the Day of Atonement) were lovely: walking up and down Park Avenue, you saw everybody you wanted to see.

It wasn't all rosy. There was antisemitism everywhere. But one simply avoided the local bullies and bigots of all stripes. By the same token, friendships were meaningful. There were no Facebook friends back then. If you called on someone, you knew you could depend on them.

Competition was always in play. At Baron Byng, students quickly learned that if you wanted to be heard, you had to assert yourself. Whether you succeeded or not depended on you. If you weren't good at something, there was a sense that you should get out of the way; there were others who would be better than you at that activity. And yet one of the nice things for such a concentrated, competitive environment was that no one was consciously excluded.

Some teachers at Baron Byng were awful, some were extraordinary. O. J. (Yos) Lummis, who taught physics and was a conscientious teacher, could barely see or hear. Mr. Cameron was a superb math teacher. I remember Walter Herring's amazing readings of Shakespeare to this day. Anne Savage was an inspiring teacher of art and a world-class artist in her own right whose paintings can be found in every major gallery of Canadian art. There were no formal music classes, but somewhere along the line most students developed a love of music and dance.

Evelyn Gold, *Echoes*. The title of Ev's painting is inspired by the Baron Byng yearbook, *The Echo*.

But the person at Baron Byng whom I remember best is Mr. Henderson, the principal. A year or two into high school, and periodically after that, he called me into his office to talk about my future. Today he might be called a guidance counsellor, helping students make decisions about what university to attend, but back then the role was not common. Being spoken to respectfully and seriously by the principal meant a lot at the time, and those discussions with Mr. Henderson encouraged me immensely. Long after I had left Baron Byng, we exchanged holiday cards, and he always made sure to invite me back to the holiday music festival.

We had more options than our parents, and that required decisions. The options were to get good marks and continue studies in university—or to join the "Jewish Navy," as it was called back then, and become a shipper in

Baron Byng graduates of 1953, with Principal Henderson and other teachers across the top row. I am in the centre (class president) and my "lieutenants" Sam Borenstein and Morris Schwisberg are centre right.

the schmatte trade. In other words: keep learning and head for something exciting, or start sweating with no great future. I knew which path I wanted to take.

We took Baron Byng with us to McGill University, Sir George Williams (now Concordia University), and onward into the world. We floated into careers at first, like all young people, but when we decided on a field where we wanted to be, we anchored ourselves. "Better to be a good plumber than a bad doctor," my father once said, and that was the prevailing attitude growing up on the Plateau: find something you're good at and do it well. Whatever that thing was, we put our lives into it and let people know, quietly and pleasantly, that we were there. Baron Byngers were prepared to do this.

In 1980, Baron Byng closed. New immigrant communities, such as the Portuguese and Greek, followed the Jewish wave (which had largely moved north and west of Montreal by then). Indeed, I met many Baron Byngers from those communities at McGill and beyond years later. But with the switch to French-language schooling in the wake of Quebec's Bill 101, Baron Byng was apparently no longer needed to serve the neighbourhood's educational needs. Thankfully, Sid Stevens, a Baron Byng alumnus, stepped forward and the building became the home base for Sun Youth, a support organization that provides families across the city with food, clothing, sports equipment, day camps, books, and more.

In 2018, the English Montreal School Board announced that local demand for an English-language high school had shifted once again, and that Baron Byng would be renovated and re-opened in the coming decade. Plus ça change…

On the Waterfront

Back when Saint Lawrence Boulevard was a two-way street, the Number 55 streetcar that trundled past our home ran all the way south to the harbour. Starting in high school, I would hop on and take it down to the waterfront, whenever I had the urge, and watch the longshoremen loading and unloading boats on the docks. The cost of my tram ride, after I got to know some of the conductors, went from 5¢ (the student rate) down to a wink and a nod.

I liked the harbour because it was different: the wind blowing in off the river carried the sounds of fifty languages and the thrill of a wider world beyond. I went there often enough that one group of longshoremen adopted me, giving me the nickname "le petit juif" (no insult intended), and let me hang around with them. They explained what "Use No Hooks" meant, gave me a hook of my own, and let me help unload smaller items on occasion. I also started to understand the chuckles when someone said a missing crate "must have fallen off the back of a truck."

Longshoremen had a bad reputation back then: they looked rough and ready in their overalls, rolled-up sleeves, and caps; and most people considered them lazy teamsters always threatening to go on strike. After spending time on the docks, I found the opposite: hard-working, lighthearted men who just wanted a decent wage to support their families. Moving freight is not easy work. I never encountered the shifty, corrupt bosses of *On the Waterfront*, nor any Marlon Brando types saying, "I coulda been a contenda."

As an undergraduate at McGill, I stopped visiting the docks as the curriculum became more intense and my free time more limited. But after I started practising medicine in 1968, one of the longshoremen I had met on the docks, Ray Joly, became a patient of mine at the Montreal General.

Some years later, I had a meeting with the hospital's CEO, Harvey Barkun, about getting television sets installed in the Radiation Oncology Centre. Cancer patients from all over the city would regularly come to the radiation centre at the Montreal General, and I found it disturbing there was nothing to occupy them while they awaited therapy.

Harvey agreed.

OPPOSITE: *Two Men, Port of Montreal* by Paul-Marc Auger, 1938. The cold-storage facility in the background was among the largest in the world at the time.

ABOVE LEFT: Unloading molasses from CNSS *Challenger*, Port of Montreal, 1947.

ABOVE RIGHT: Unloading bananas from the Caribbean from the steamship *Lady Rodney*, for shipment by train across Canada.

"But, Phil," he said, "there are no funds available right now for this."

As fate would have it, immediately after my meeting with Harvey, my next patient was Ray Joly, the longshoreman. I must have looked upset because he asked what was bothering me. I told him about the TV sets and the lack of funding.

Three days later, I got a call from the Goods Receiving Department at the hospital.

"There are six television sets here with your name on them, Dr. Gold," said a voice. "Where do you want them?"

Fighting the desire to say "Radiation Oncology," I insisted they be returned—only to learn there was no return address listed.

I called my old friend and explained that I couldn't accept anything that had "fallen off the back of a truck"—grateful as I was for his efforts. Later that day, four of the TV sets were removed from the hospital. The remaining two sat around unopened—and were eventually installed in Radiation Oncology. Ray Joly's efforts were, indeed, appreciated, and the patients were happier.

Summer Jobs

Throughout my teenage years and early twenties, I always had different summer jobs. Here are some distinct memories from a number of them.

Pearl's Grocery
The summer after grade eight, I was looking for a job to augment my rather modest weekly allowance. Walking down the Main, I passed Pearl's Grocery. A card in the window read:

> GOING OUT OF BUSINESS
> Boy wanted to help complete
> the sale of all remaining groceries

Selling groceries for a dollar an hour seemed a fine way to spend a couple of weeks. I inquired inside. The manager took one look at me—I had been lifting weights at the Y since I was around twelve years old—and hired me on the spot.

As it turned out, I wasn't exactly selling groceries, I was schlepping (dragging) them. I was, in fact, Head Schlepper of sacks and boxes from the basement storage room, up the narrow stairs, and onto the shelves.

Well, good exercise! I told myself.

As the weeks passed, however, the inventory never seemed to grow smaller. One morning when I arrived earlier than usual, I learned why: from a truck in the back, two men were unloading a fresh supply of dry and canned goods. Pearl's was prolonging the action. This brought to mind a cartoon I had seen in *The New Yorker* of a father and son standing on the sidewalk outside his store, with a *Going Out of Business* sign in the window. "One day, my boy," says the father, "all this will be yours."

And so the job I had thought might go a few weeks ended up lasting all summer. I became a wealthy teenager. Come September, I still had almost $250 stashed in a box beside my bed.

I was also in great shape. Friends asked, "Have you been lifting weights?" And, indeed, I kept lifting weights at the Y for another half-dozen years or so, until the busy schedule of medical school took over my days.

Faye Perm
By the next summer—Pearl's Grocery had finally gone out of business—I saw an advertisement in the *Montreal Herald*:

> HELP WANTED
> A student for all-purpose work
> Inquire at Faye Perm Displays
> 8 St. Catherine St. East
> Montreal 18, Que.

LEFT: Workers in the original Steinberg's grocery store at 4419 St. Lawrence, with Ida Steinberg sitting behind cash, 1920s.

RIGHT: A Montreal Tramways Company street trolley, early 1940s. The flaming sword on the side is a government ad encouraging citizens to invest in Victory Bonds. The city's trolley era ended in 1959.

The business of Faye Perm was renting mannequins to retail clothing stores. Once again my job was grunt work, only this time I was schlepping arms, legs, and torsos to and from storefronts along Saint Catherine Street, and anywhere else within walking distance.

My years of weight training proved invaluable: the mannequins were very heavy, especially the bases and stands. The newer models had castor wheels so I could push them, but a wheel or two was often broken. I asked the manager one day why they didn't use a truck for delivery.

"You're cheaper than a truck," he said.

I lugged mannequins around downtown through the heat of summer for another six weeks until I nearly fainted one day from the exertion. I went into a pharmacy and asked for a glass of water. When I went back out, I noticed the pharmacy's thermometer read 105 Fahrenheit (40 Celsius).

I gave notice that afternoon. My holidays started the next day.

The DEW Line and Urban Camp

The summer after grade ten, Mort Levy and I decided to apply for summer jobs on the Distant Early Warning (DEW) Line. The DEW Line was a system of radar observation stations along the shores of the Arctic Ocean, in the Northwest Territories, set up to defend against potential Soviet bombers during the Cold War. Happily, nothing like this ever occurred.

At what were probably the main offices of the Department of National Defence in Montreal, Mort and I took a written exam with a dozen other young men applying for the job. We finished in short order, handed in our tests, and then went home to await the outcome of our jobs on the DEW Line.

Mort remembers that we did better on the exam than anyone else, and to this day he insists we would have gotten the jobs. Personally, I think we finished the test too quickly and may have seemed too smart for our own good.

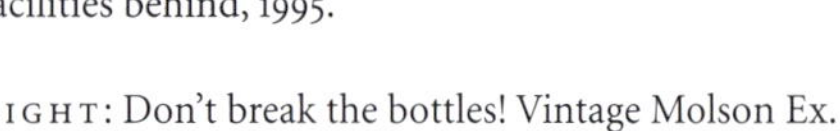

LEFT: Molson Brewery's stone façade, with larger modern facilities behind, 1995.

RIGHT: Don't break the bottles! Vintage Molson Ex.

Regardless of the result, when our mothers got wind of our initiative, they immediately put the kibosh on our plan. No sons of theirs were going off to the Northwest Territories to take part in some *meshugas* (craziness).

The next day, as Mort and I sat bemoaning our fates in the coffee shop of the Y, in comes Ralph Garber. Ralph, a social worker, was the activities director at the YMHA and a terrific guy we'd known for years. Indeed, he would go on to be the dean of social work at the University of Toronto.

"Hey, boys. Whatcha doing this summer?"

We explained how our mothers wouldn't let us work on the DEW Line, even if we had gotten the jobs.

"Would you consider being camp counsellors?" asked Ralph.

The Y was starting up a new Urban Camp, he said, for all the kids who couldn't get out of the city but who still needed something fun and energetic to do. And so began three or four enjoyable summers for both of us as Urban Camp counsellors and eventually head counsellors.

Molson Brewery

The summer after grade eleven, before our freshman year at McGill, we got lucky again. Mort's father owned an early form of a depanneur on Notre Dame Street and he learned from his supplier at Molson that the brewery was hiring summer workers. We applied, got jobs, and the hours were perfect. Urban Camp ran from 8 a.m. to 3 p.m., and the streetcar took us straight down Park Avenue and over to the brewery for the 4 p.m.-to-midnight shift. After a few weeks, Mort didn't care for the boredom of the work on the loading dock so he started delivering groceries for his dad instead. But I was happy to be a "washed-bottle watcher." It's amazing what people put in bottles, from cigarette butts (easy enough) to a mouse (which I never figured out). For $60/week, I checked bottles that were downloaded in rows onto what was called a "piano," and if every bottle was empty of debris and washed clean, they were moved onto a conveyor belt for refilling. The only rule: Don't break the bottles! Beer is cheap, but the bottles were 17 cents each. The task was easy, so while I worked I would do geometry and trigonometry problems in my head to keep myself entertained. And when the shift ended there was free beer. Many workers stayed to drink and share a few laughs. My fellow workers came from different backgrounds, but we all appreciated the camaraderie. Most nights I even made it home to get some sleep before Urban Camp started the next morning. But I must have had my fill of beer for a lifetime, or the taste of beer stopped appealing to me, because I haven't had a beer in all the years since then.

Selling Encyclopedias

In the second of my two summers at Molson, I added yet another job to my schedule: selling the *Encyclopaedia Britannica Junior* on weekends. The pay was a flat-rate commission of $23 per set sold and I worked with three older salesmen, going from district to district around the city. I came to enjoy, immensely, the company and good humour of the veteran salesmen, in particular a delightful Spaniard, José Garcia, who taught me how to give the sales pitch. José was a natural salesman and after running me through the routine, he assured me that I'd do well. After four hours of door-to-door cold calls (a finger on the doorbell, a foot in the door), we would meet back at the car and have a snack together. The group was genuinely happy for anyone who made a sale and they really celebrated when "the kid" (me) made his first sale.

One evening in Greenfield Park I was invited into a home. I strolled into the living room to start my pitch, whereupon I tripped on the carpet, fell over, dropped my briefcase, and spilled its entire contents across the floor. Embarrassed, I gathered my materials, apologized for wasting the couple's time, and was about to leave when the woman of the house, seeing that I was upset, offered me "a nice cup of tea." I accepted and, after a bit of conversation with her and her husband, they bought a set of encyclopedias for their children. From that evening on I tripped my way across the threshold of every home in Greenfield Park. If something works, use it!

Partway through the summer, I quit my bottle-watching duties so I could sell encyclopedias every evening. The experience taught me two important lessons. First, whether it's encyclopedias, medical concepts, or research proposals, so many things in life involve *selling*; and second, confidence is essential. Both lessons came in handy for me decades later as director of the McGill Cancer Centre, and after that as physician-in-chief at the Montreal General Hospital, when I had to engage with my colleagues and with the administration.

"Two dimes a day": the 1962 *Encyclopaedia Britannica Junior*, with its Book a Month Payment Plan. The ad on the left asks, What is more important to your child… the size of his home or the size of his mind? And on the right, Why do some families seem to get more out of life?

Leaving the Old Neighbourhood

In spring 1953 when I was sixteen, near the end of my last year at Baron Byng (grade eleven), my family moved out of the old neighbourhood and "moved up" to 2110 Bedford Road, just northwest of Outremont. Our new home was a brand-new double duplex that my parents purchased jointly with the Katz family (no relation to Evelyn's family). My parents owned the left side of the building, rented out the upper flat, and we lived downstairs.

The move was possible because Phillip Katz and my father had recently gone into business together as "jobbers," or freelance contractors. Their shift to jobbing made sense. After years in the schmatte industry working in various capacities for various employers, they had good contacts, were widely trusted, and my father had a reputation as the best sewing-machine operator in the industry.

My father and Phillip had an efficient production line with a dozen or more workers in the Sternthal Building at 1435 Saint Alexandre Street, in the heart of the clothing district just behind the Gordon Brown Building on de Maisonneuve. The company did not have a name per se and didn't need one, since the partners were so well known. They produced coats, suits, and other stylish ladies' outerwear for the upcoming season for large manufacturers, and did a lot of work for Auckie Sanft, the leading ladies' garment producer in the city. This was sophisticated tailoring that required years of expertise and a good eye, which both men possessed.

The new business gave me my first job outside the summer holidays as company jack-of-all-trades, earning $25/week, during my undergraduate years at McGill. Phillip's son, Allan, who was ahead of me at McGill studying engineering, had started doing the job but after a year or two found the work too time-consuming, so I was recruited. Allan gave me a one-hour lesson in my responsibilities and pronounced me competent.

New house, new neighbourhood: 2110 Bedford Road. We lived on the ground floor in the foreground. The Katz family (no relation to Evelyn's family) lived on the right.

There were three main parts to the job: banking, removing basting, and schlepping. In the first, I calculated the weekly income of each employee so that the specific funds obtained from the bank matched their salary pay envelope exactly, down to the last penny. If a garment cutter earned $162.43/week, for example, I would enter the requested bills and coin for the bank as follows:

1 — one-hundred-dollar bill
6 — ten-dollar bills
1 — two-dollar bill (loonies and toonies didn't exist yet)
1 — quarter
1 — dime
1 — nickel
3 — pennies

And so on for everyone at the firm. Adding it up, the bank would provide the various denominations of bills and change, which the following afternoon I would painstakingly put into individual envelopes.

The second part of the job involved taking out temporary threads called basting from garments, moving the unfinished garments from station to station in the factory, and then sweeping the shop floor. Basting thread was tricky: some of it could be removed easily, but sometimes a stitch got caught, and yanking hard could ruin the whole garment—which was unthinkable.

My third task was the most difficult physically: delivering finished garments to the manufacturers. Twice a week during the afternoons and early evenings, I schlepped heavy loads on foot from our factory to others around the downtown clothing industry district. I would carry about twenty garments at a time on my shoulder. Most destinations were within a half-dozen blocks of our shop, and most had elevators. When I arrived, a checker would inspect the garments and issue a receipt for merchandise delivered "in good condition"—meaning no rips, no grease, no mud, no snow, no unfinished stitches. In the dark of winter, I often came close to disaster, navigating the poorly lit alleyways and slippery outer stairs of the factory buildings. Again, thank goodness for the YMHA, and all my years of weightlifting there, or the task might have been overwhelming. Red-faced and out of breath, I regularly got the "friendly" comment from the checkers, "Now you know what real work is."

Looking back now, the most enjoyable aspect of those schmatte years, for me, was talking to everyone on the shop floor: the fabric cutters, the operators, the pressers. I loved to watch them perform their craft and listen to their witty, lighthearted banter. There was a sense of camaraderie in the sweatshops that is hard to find nowadays.

After a few years, my father's and Phillip Katz's business ground to a halt. They were obviously good at what they did but the market, the cost of managing the enterprise, and the responsibility probably all played a part. I'm sure the failure was a hard blow for them. Mr. Katz went back to the factories as a sewing-machine operator. My father returned to the factories as well, this time as a ladies' clothing designer, and he was an extremely good at it. In the coming years he spent a lot of time in New York, copying fashionable designs. He would take the train down to Manhattan, walk Fifth Avenue looking at garments in the windows, go inside and inspect them off the rack, examining cut, fabric, lining, and trim. After so many years in the trade, he could take a garment apart in his mind and put it back together again knowing the placement of almost every stitch inside. Back in Montreal, he would design something similar or in combination with his own ideas. When I think of the flair for design that my sister, Malk, and my daughter, Josie, possess, I know from whence it came.

Watching my father's business grow and fail, I saw how hard he and his confreres had to work just to put food on the table. And even in my part-time capacity I felt the work's drudgery and boredom deep in my bones. This was *not* how I wanted to spend my life.

My parents had arrived in Canada with nothing and made something of themselves, like so many others, so that their children could choose their

The Sternthal Building at 1435 Saint Alexandre, with its art-deco lettering and stylish marble entryway. Thank goodness for elevators. Dad and Phillip Katz's company was on the fourth floor.

careers and direction in life freely. And as my mother said, she felt fortunate: she had escaped the lethal antisemitism of her native land and wasn't chattel to anyone. Knowing what they had gone through, I couldn't let them down. In the words of Saul Bellow, I had to seize the day. At Baron Byng I'd witnessed what happened to students who didn't go on to university: many of them joined the "Jewish Navy" of shippers and manual labourers in the schmatte industry right out of high school. For many years my parents had made clear their wish that I become a physician. "Our son the doctor," they would say. I had no desire to study medicine, but I was determined to have choices in life. University was the clear path toward those choices.

First Car

At some point after our move uptown to Bedford Road, my father bought our first car, a 1953 Pontiac (which my father liked to kid around and mispronounce "Ponchiak"). Phillip Katz also bought a '53 Pontiac. Ours was light brown. Theirs was blue.

By the time I was a teenager I had already learned how to drive, quite illegally, with my friend Morris Cohen in his father's butcher truck. Morris lived on Hutchison and when his father wasn't around we used to slowly roll around the Plateau, hoping not to hurt anyone or be stopped by police. The truck had an eight-gear floor shift, and it was a great way to learn how

RIGHT: 1953 Pontiac four-door sedan. My father liked to kid around and pronounce it "Ponchiak." Ours was light brown, the Katzes' was blue.

OPPOSITE: Evelyn Gold, *A Cherry Drink*, her painting of Wilensky's Light Luncheon on Fairmount.

to drive and use a clutch. Truth be told, we weren't too concerned about getting caught. The local officers knew who we were and one time even nodded at us from their car as we drove past them.

I have no idea how, or when, my father learned to drive—he probably learned from a friend just before buying the car—but once I had my licence he gave me tips on handling the wheel-mounted gearshift. Parking was a strenuous activity before the advent of power steering, and also had to be practised. On Saturday nights, if I had a date, my father would often let me take out the car, a trusting and very nice gesture in a one-car family. I picked up Evelyn for our first date in that '53 Pontiac.

In the 1980s, when I taught my son Ian to drive, I made sure that he could handle a manual stick shift first. Josie and Joel then learned manual from Ian. Josie still drives a manual today and loves it!

Phil Gold, Baron Byng graduation, spring 1953.

PART II

Through the Roddick Gates

McGill and Beyond

After four years of high school, Mort and I and a bunch of other Baron Byng grads found our way to McGill University.

McGill faces onto Sherbrooke Street, fronted by the beautifully designed Roddick Gates, an architectural semicircle of stone and wrought iron. The gates were named for Sir Thomas George Roddick, a renowned doctor at the Montreal General Hospital and later dean (1901–08) of the Faculty of Medicine.

That September 1953, Mort insisted we enter through the open gates. Back then, the gates were only opened on special occasions, for example, the day after Labour Day, the traditional start of the fall semester.

With the library and science wings on either side, and the Arts building in front, its cupola framed by the Mountain, entering the McGill campus is inspiring. And for Jewish students back then who required significantly higher marks to gain admission, getting into McGill held an extra sense of achievement.

Walking through the gates, I had the strangest urge.

"Mort," I said, "I'm going to leave this place better than I found it."

Mort, being Mort, shrugged. Like Atlas, he's pragmatic.

My euphoria was short-lived, pushed aside by the pressing question: what will we study now that we're here? Planning ahead is not a teenager's strong suit.

We decided to pool our efforts. Mort would go to a geology lecture and I'd see what zoology had to offer.

A few hours later, we met for lunch.

"How was the zoology lecture?" asked Mort.

"Bloody awful," I said, "he droned on and on. Lousy lecturer."

Hand-coloured postcard of the Roddick Gates in high summer, with clock set into the left tower. The gates were built in 1925 by Amy Redpath Roddick in memory of her husband Sir Thomas Roddick, a renowned doctor at the General who became dean of the Faculty of Medicine at McGill.

"Who was the prof?"

"Some guy named Berrill." Professor N. J. Berrill, I later learned, was a giant in the field of invertebrate zoology.

"How was geology?" I asked.

"Honestly, it was great," said Mort. "But there's a hooker. Mandatory Saturday-morning field trips."

And that's why we picked courses in biology: so we could sleep in on Saturday mornings. And our lifelong directions evolved from that point on! Talk about the fortunome (more on that later).

During my years at McGill, I experienced a white-collar variety of antisemitism to match the blue-collar brand I had faced down on the streets of the Plateau. It was not as blatant, but it certainly existed and was supported by the university's longstanding system of limiting the number of Jewish students who could attend. For example, the Faculties of Medicine and Law restricted Jewish enrolment to 10 percent.

But it's what we encountered among fellow students that hurt the most. Chatting happily in groups on campus, someone would make an inadvertent comment like "Jews are just everywhere here," perhaps without realizing the pain that might cause to the Jews in the group. Or perhaps intending it.

One Jewish friend described this as "a hand on your shoulder and a knife in your back."

Why were these students so hostile? Those who've read the novels of Mordecai Richler, a late friend and fellow Baron Bynger, may remember a passage in *Joshua Then and Now* in which news arrives that Joshua's brother-in-law has committed suicide. Joshua asks his wife why her brother would do such a thing. He had everything going for him!

Road trip to the Stratford Festival, summer 1955. From left: me, Mort, Wilkie Kushner, and Mel Month. The night we got there it was pouring rain. After we put up our tent, Mort poked the canvas to check how heavy the rain was. The lake that formed on the tent floor confirmed it was heavy. Never touch a wet tent from the inside!

Her explanation is telling. All his life, she says, her brother had been the fair-haired boy from the best family, the tennis champ at the club, always first in his class, and desired by the girls. But when he got to McGill, he met a bunch of dark-eyed, dark-haired boys who didn't give a damn about his family or his background. He had to gain their respect, she explains, but things had been given to him his whole life, he hadn't been raised to make himself heard, and he couldn't work as hard as they did. The competition overwhelmed him.

The passage accurately reflects the flavour of antisemitism at McGill when we arrived. That changed quickly in the next decade, only to return again a half-century later. Antisemitism has great staying power.

Meeting Arnold

In our second year at McGill, Mort and I both chose to major in honours physiology, along with Irwin (Korny) Kornbluth and Tom Min Swi Chang. The golden age of any department is usually deemed to be in some hoary decade past, but for the four of us it was right there in front of us. There was department chair Frank C. (Hank) MacIntosh, who had performed outstanding studies on neural transmission; Benedict Delisle (Ben) Burns, who did remarkable work on neural networks using isolated brain slabs; electrophysiologist Paul Sekelj, who narrowly escaped the Nazis in Vienna in 1938 before inventing, among other things, one of the first whole-blood oximeters for clinical use; and then there was Arnold Stanley Vincent Burgen, the only true genius I've ever known.

LEFT: The James Biology building, now the university's Administration building, where I took physiology courses and began my study of erythropoietin. If you go there today, the regal-looking frog above the main door is the only clue to the building's original purpose.

RIGHT: Portrait of Sir Arnold Burgen, Darwin College, University of Cambridge, by June Mendoza.

We had a ball. My three years of studying physiology were what a university experience should be. There was never a whiff of antisemitism from anyone in the department and, with only four students in our year, we got to know our professors very well, and vice versa.

My mentor Arnold Burgen and I developed an affinity early on. I remember the first time I saw Arnold, in the fourth-floor hallway of the James Biology building, his head was tilted to one side. He nodded to me, recognizing one of the four new kids on the block. He taught our introductory classes in physiology that year and led subsequent classes and labs involving the four of us for the next three years. During those sessions he showed us, quite literally, the future of biomedical science. He explained experiments that were yet to be done, important questions that still needed answers, and his predictions were right on the mark. Had Arnold had the patience to stay within one area of endeavour he would certainly have received a Nobel Prize for so much of the work that he started. As it was, when he later returned to Cambridge, he held many posts, including Sheild Professor of Pharmacology, master of Darwin College, and then director of the National Institute for Medical Research at Mill Hill—England's leading medical research institute—where his impact deepened and spread, and for which he was knighted in 1976. Sir Arnold Burgen is also the founding president of Academia Europaea.

But I'm getting ahead of myself. Arnold was recruited by Hank MacIntosh, who was in England doing a fellowship with Sir Henry Dale. As the story goes, Arnold had trained as a pediatrician and found working with sick children emotionally difficult. Apparently, discussing the matter in the London Underground one day, Hank said to Arnold, I'm going back to Montreal soon, would you like to come with me? Arnold said yes, came to Montreal, and became a professor in the Physiology Department at McGill.

Arnold was a remarkable intellect but also great fun. On one exam approaching the New Year's break, he'd added a fairly impossible question at the end of the test. I wrote: "It's a great question, but only G-d knows the answer. Merry Christmas." When I got my exam back, Arnold's response was, "God gets 100 and you get Zero. Happy New Year."

It's no exaggeration to say working with a scientist of Burgen's stature changed my life. In my final year in physiology, he supervised my research project into erythropoietin, in which I began to devise methods for altering the production of the molecule and other methods to measure its concentration. Erythropoietin is a hormone produced largely by the kidneys. It acts on the bone marrow to control the production of red blood cells (erythrocytes). At high altitudes, for example, there is a greater need for the oxygen-carrying hemoglobin of erythrocytes and so more erythropoietin is produced to stimulate the production of erythrocytes.

Erythropoietin became an important molecule in the treatment of anemia, so the hormone became a drug, some years later. I continued to study it for four more summers during medical school and enjoyed access to Arnold's brilliant mind until I completed my M.Sc. degree.

Nowadays when I give lectures in physiology, sometimes to classes of over a thousand students, I feel a little sorry. The great majority of them will never have the opportunities that I had as an undergraduate.

Career Paths, Taken and Not Taken

Two roads diverged in a yellow wood,
And sorry I could not travel both
And be one traveler, long I stood
And looked down one as far as I could
To where it bent in the undergrowth;
Then took the other, as just as fair,
And having perhaps the better claim,
Because it was grassy and wanted wear [...]

—Robert Frost, "The Road Not Taken"

The Strathcona Medical Building. "Are you coming up to sign your application forms?"

It was not my intent to be a physician.

But I became one, and I've had a pretty successful career. Why did I take this path, and not another?

As Frost's poem suggests, reasons that appear to be intentional in retrospect are often, in the moment of choosing, somewhat random. My life is no exception!

Here are a few thoughts.

One reason I chose medicine may be because my parents *wanted* me to be a physician. "Our son the doctor," they sometimes said. (As the mother in the old joke says, "Help! Help! My son the doctor is drowning!") But like most immigrants who'd worked their whole lives just to put food on the table, my parents would have been happy with pretty much any career I chose so long as it was a white-collar profession at which I was successful.

So my parents' hopes did not carry that much weight when I started at McGill in the fall of 1953. Like my son Joel's reasons for picking Brown over Harvard and Yale, the reasons Mort and I chose the biological sciences in our first year were entirely idiosyncratic. As I mentioned, if McGill's Geology Department hadn't scheduled its field trips for Saturday mornings, we might have wound up as geologists. Instead we chose physiology, alongside Korny and Tom, we had the experience of a lifetime in a world-class department, and all four of us subsequently went on to medical school. Mort specialized in nephrology at the Royal Victoria, Irwin became an obstetrician, and Tom

Physiology graduates, 1957: Irwin Kornbluth, Phil Gold, Eleonor Gondor, Mort Levy, Tom Chang. Eleonor graduated alongside us in physiology but was not in the honours program.

turned his undergraduate investigations of microcapsules into a lifetime of important research.

And yet even in March 1957, six months before I began medical school, I had no intention of choosing medicine. I had a different plan: to continue my research of the hormone erythropoietin, which I had started to study as a final-year project under my brilliant mentor Arnold Burgen, and to work toward a Ph.D. in physiology.

But one day that spring, Arnold called me into his office.

"You know, Phil," he said, "a few years of medical school would do you a great deal of good."

I told him I had other plans.

"You don't need to complete the whole degree, just the first two years. Two years should expand your knowledge of human biology sufficiently." This, he explained, would allow me to take my erythropoietin research to a Ph.D. level. I told him I'd go home and think about it.

A few days later, I got a call from Merle Peden, the secretary of the School of Medicine.

"Hello, is this Phillip Gold?" she asked.

"Phil Gold, yes, speaking."

"Are you coming up to sign your application forms?"

"What forms?"

"For medical school. Dr. Burgen said you had to sign them."

ABOVE: Evelyn as a teenager, Trout Lake, 1953.

OPPOSITE: This is my favourite portrait of Ev.

Arnold, what have you done? I thought.

"All right," I said, "I'll come by later this morning."

Not quite sure what I was doing, or why, I went over to the Strathcona building and found myself signing the application forms for the McGill Faculty of Medicine.

I may have backed into it, but medical school turned out to be a great path. I excelled there—and did so without giving up on my own interests: I continued to study erythropoietin during the summers, under Arnold's guidance, at the University Medical Clinic (UMC) of the Montreal General Hospital, where Arnold was the new deputy director. I even received a decent summer stipend.

My Two Chances with Evelyn Katz

In the spring of 1957, during my last semester of physiology, I met an extremely attractive young woman at a party thrown by an acquaintance, Morty Schiff. It was a large party with the usual contingent of pseudo-intellectuals taking their talking points from *Newsweek* or *Time* magazine, and at one point I had to strongly disagree with the maven of the evening, who was making a hash of the philosophy of Nietzsche. My own opinions had developed during long summer discussions with an acquaintance, Herbie Lewis, who had written his Ph.D. thesis on the German philosopher.

Neither I nor the attractive young woman were impressed by the conversation, so the two of us peeled off to talk alone, away from the madding crowd. We talked for quite a long time, me slowly drinking rye. We got along very well indeed. As the noisy party wound down, I got her number and said I'd call soon to get together again, hopefully somewhere quieter.

Love Always
Evelyn

LEFT: Evelyn Gold, *Changes*. This is the door where I picked up Ev for our not-so-blind first date, December 1957.

RIGHT: A photo from another wedding we attended during our dating years.

When I awoke the next day, I remembered the young lady and our pleasant conversation—but for the life of me, I couldn't remember her name or phone number. I asked some friends who she was, but it had been a large, raucous party and they couldn't say. Days turned to weeks. Final exams appeared on the horizon. My thoughts turned to other matters.

But I never really forgot her.

Some nine months later, over the December break—by this point I was in medical school—I got a call from a classmate, David Schiff, asking for a favour. He said his cousin needed someone to accompany her to a friend's wedding. She hadn't planned to attend because of a family holiday in Florida, but the poor weather down south had ended her family's vacation early and she was back in town and needed someone to go with her. He'd tried my line with no answer, and then he called Mort Levy and Irwin Kornbluth, both of whom were busy. Was I free?

After an intense first semester of medical school, I was tired of books—and my mother was clearly growing sick of me hanging around the house all day.

I said I'd be happy to go.

LEFT: Poster for an exhibition of the Plasticiens, 1955.

RIGHT: The sign outside L'Échourie in 1954, from the National Film Board documentary *Artist in Montreal.*

David gave me his cousin's address at 5040 Borden Avenue, and a few days later I drove my father's Pontiac over to the house and rang the bell.

The door opened and there she was—the beautiful person from the party!

"Ev," I said, quickly feigning some knowledge of the situation, "I'm late, but here I am!"

Her name was Evelyn Katz.

She was, as I remembered her from the party, a total knockout, this time in an extraordinary green dress.

But rather than appreciate my incredibly good luck in getting a second chance with her, I couldn't help noticing she had put on a great deal of makeup. Being the romantic guy that I am, I suggested she go back inside and wash her face. In retrospect, I can't believe that I said that. It was idiotic—but I survived.

Evelyn, to her credit, did not push me down the stairs and slam the door in my face. She simply excused herself to go and redo her makeup.

Evelyn's mother came to the door.

"Hello, my name is Phil Gold," I said, shaking her hand.

Evelyn's mother, impressed that I had offered to shake her hand, which none of her daughter's previous dates had done, stayed at the door and talked with me for a few minutes. According to Evelyn, by the end of our conversation, her mother (Bubbie Chanah) was ready to call a rabbi and rent a shul for the wedding.

Evelyn Gold, *IT-L-DO*, the Katz family cottage on Trout Lake.

Evelyn returned, her lovely face and natural beauty now wonderfully apparent. We went to her friend's wedding, had a lovely time, and continued the evening at L'Échourie, a trendy resto-bar-gallery on Pine Avenue near Clark.

Today, Evelyn maintains that the makeup was part of her "rebellious" phase and describes my words before our not-so-blind first date as "absolutely charming." But, she adds, in a twenty-first-century context, my comments might well deserve a push down the stairs!

From the vantage point of sixty years, I realize my great good fortune. I have spent my entire adult life with someone I love. Beautiful and talented, Evelyn has been the mainstay of my life. We've disagreed at times, about everything from how to raise our children to the colour of my tie, but there have only been a handful of nights we went to bed angry with each other. She is the only woman I have ever loved, and I was extraordinarily fortunate to find her.

I have two pieces of advice for my grandchildren and anyone else reading this. First, if you intend to drink, please arrange for a taxi, bus, or designated driver to get you home. And second, when you meet "the one," don't forget their name and number! Write it down!

Evelyn, me, Bubbie Chana, Clara and Murray Silver. We still miss Murray today.

Dating Evelyn

Over the next three years, Ev and I dated and fell in love.

Like me, Evelyn was a first-generation Canadian. Her father, Joseph (Yudel) Katz, and her mother, Chana (Annie) Schiff, had emigrated as young people from Eastern Europe, met in Montreal, and gotten married. Like me, she had grown up in the old neighbourhood, at 5377 Saint Urbain, until the age of ten and had fond memories of eating lunch at Wilensky's with her father. Joe was a talented carpenter who started a furniture-frame company, City Furniture, with Chana's encouragement. They had two daughters. Ev's older sister, Clara, took after their father and by her late teens was his business confidante, sharing in the planning and worries as the precarious enterprise grew. Indeed, she started to work at the company and remained there for decades. Evelyn remembers her father calculating the day's revenues and expenses on a napkin at the dinner table, double-checking every night that he was still in the black, a habit she picked up from him.

City Furniture eventually became very successful, but the chronic financial concern shaped Clara, adding a layer of anxiety to her personality. Evelyn, perhaps because she was six years younger, and certainly of a more naturally cheerful and optimistic demeanour, didn't experience the same angst.

In 1952, when Clara was nineteen, she married Murray Silver, one of the most charming, outgoing, and optimistic people one could ever hope to know. For teenage Evelyn, the addition of Murray made the Katz family feel complete. Murray was the brother she never had. Indeed, Murray was everyone's brother. Clara and Murray had three children: Elaine, Howard, and Steven.

Murray passed away in 1989 of heart disease, and we still miss him. He was a wonderful guy.

After Murray died, Clara was left bereft as she struggled to get back to her life and her family. It was painful to watch such a good sister and a good friend suffer as she did.

Once Evelyn and I started dating, the rest of her family welcomed me immediately with open arms, inviting me to their cottage on Trout Lake, called IT-L-DO—the words proclaimed on a wooden post beside the front walk—for extended stays during the summer of 1958. Indeed, they even let me spend a week there alone that August to study in seclusion for an upcoming course in pathology. That was the same week, incidentally, that I began the bad habit of smoking. More on that later.

My own family life contrasted starkly with Evelyn's. My mother was a warm and loving person, but she had raised me effectively on her own, with little input from my emotionally distant father. As I grew into my twenties, she became more and more possessive. No one was good enough for her Phil. As a result, Evelyn never felt welcomed into our family. Up until then I'd gone on plenty of dates, so my mother was delighted that I had a steady girlfriend—but when the moment came for her to share her son, she became more possessive, not less, and in many ways withheld complete acceptance of Evelyn as a true member of our family. I have never forgiven myself for allowing this distressing behaviour to continue unchecked for too long.

The Society Doctor

In January 1958, just after the New Year break during my first year of medical school, I developed fever, fatigue, and generalized malaise. A classmate also noticed lumps on my neck. When my symptoms didn't go away, my mother thought it wise to call the doctor.

In the days before universal, publicly funded Medicare became law in 1970, Canada's patchwork healthcare system included company or "society" doctors who came with the job, so to speak. As a member of the International Ladies' Garment Workers' Union (ILGWU), my father paid a regular fee for basic care for himself and immediate family members.

The lanky society doctor arrived at our door the next day in his fedora and asked to see the patient. My mother brought him to my room. Without saying hello or asking my name, and without giving his own, he strode for-

Graduation, graduation, graduation!

LEFT: My Ph.D. convocation on the McGill campus, 1965. Ev was five months pregnant at the time with Josie.

RIGHT: Ev and me in fall 1961, after my two-degree ceremony (MD, M.Sc.). Ev is holding my convocation robes while I fiddle with my camera and my mother looks on.

ward, stuck a thermometer in my mouth, grabbed my wrist, and started taking my pulse.

"You have a fever," he stated flatly.

"Yes, I do," I said, thinking, *I could have told you that.*

"My son is a medical student," said my mother proudly with a smile. "At McGill."

The doctor launched into a physical examination—still without the slightest idea of why he had been called— and examined my head and neck.

"You have enlarged cervical lymph nodes," he said, using some professional terminology.

The notion that I was a medical student must have sunk in.

"Uh-huh," I said, acknowledging another fact the patient could have told him, had he asked.

Pleased with himself, he continued without taking a medical history.

"Your chest is clear," he said, putting down his stethoscope.

Now came the *pièce de résistance*. Examining my abdomen, he announced that both my spleen and liver were enlarged.

"My G-d," said my mother, covering her face with her hands, "what does this mean?"

"Mrs. Gold," he said with a sparkle in his eye, "your son has either mononucleosis or acute leukemia."

Premier Maurice Duplessis lays the ceremonial first stone of the Montreal General Hospital in 1953.

My mother proceeded to pass out, standing in the middle of my bedroom. Thankfully the society doctor had good reflexes and caught her before her head hit the floor.

After we revived my mother—there were now two patients in the room—the society doctor announced he would take a blood sample from me and call us with the results. Perhaps knowing he had crossed the line, he showed himself out.

For the rest of the day, my mother remained in an unrelenting state of panic until Evelyn came to the house that evening and reassured her that it was almost certainly just mononucleosis. Evelyn knew of at least two other cases among friends, she said, and she was sure that was my problem.

Soon enough the results of the blood work came back, showing mononucleosis.

I stayed home for the next six weeks in bed, the prescribed cure at the time. Really a special treat. I could go to the university for exams but only if I travelled there and back by cab.

Lessons from the society doctor have remained with me throughout my life. First, ask the right questions. Second, don't cause unnecessary panic. And finally, keep your words soft and sweet. You may have to eat them!

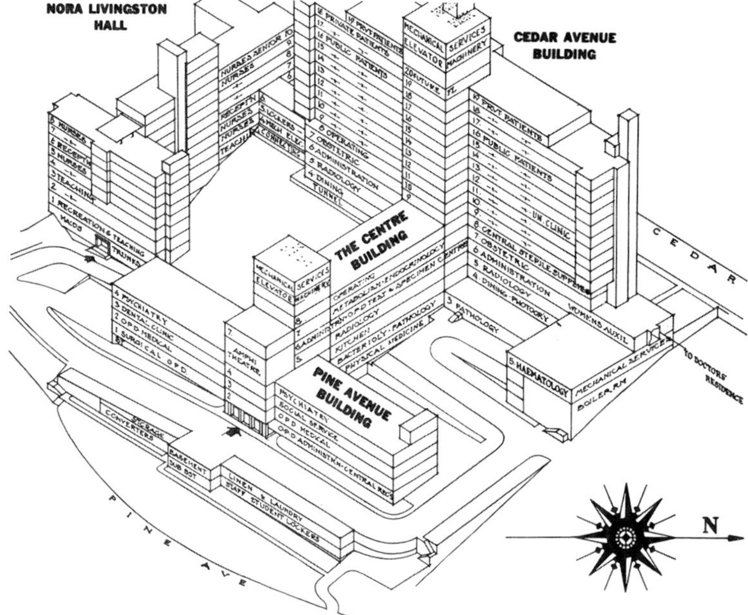

Isometric plan of the Montreal General Hospital from 1950.

Mrs. Cleghorn and the Montreal General Hospital

One memory from July 1959 has stayed with me. I was doing my summer research and experiments, as usual, in the biology building, now the James Administrative Building, on the McGill campus.

One morning, Arnold Burgen stuck his head around the door.

"We're moving," he said.

"What? Where to?" I asked.

"To the new Montreal General Hospital."

I had no idea where the hospital was, let alone that it was "new." I had never been there. Medical services, like everything else back then, were organized along ethnic and religious lines. The Montreal General Hospital, as I would learn, did not have a large Jewish staff or patient clientele.

"When are we moving?"

"In about an hour," he said. "Take what you need for the next few days. We'll come back for the rest on the weekend."

The morning became a blur as I broke down the different pieces of apparatus that had taken some time to put together and made arrangements to transfer two dozen rabbits from the animal house. Then I packed up what I could and drove with Arnold to nearby Cedar Avenue, just west of McGill. The hospital had relocated up the hill four years earlier, from Atwater and Dorchester, into a brand-new building on the slope of Mount Royal. I would

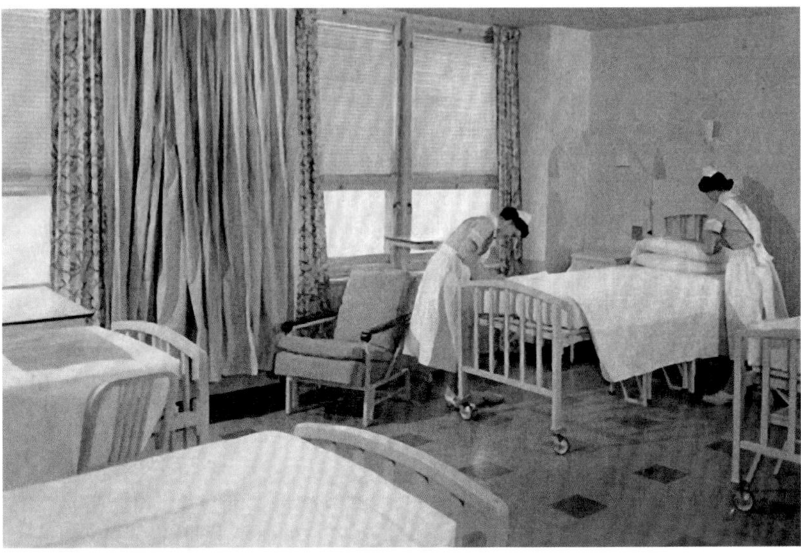

A typical four-bed ward in the new Montreal General in 1955: bright, spacious, private, and less infectious than the old sixteen-bed wards. There were also double and single rooms available, for a price.

learn that the General was really the founding institution of the McGill School of Medicine, and one of the oldest hospitals in North America, which celebrated its bicentennial in 2021.

That first day, however, exhausted, I deposited my essentials in the new space of the University Medical Clinic (UMC) on the twelfth floor. I was the only person working there that summer.

"Will you be going to the cafeteria for lunch?" Arnold asked.

"After a morning like this, yes," I replied.

Then Arnold looked me up and down and commented on my personal attire—jeans and a T-shirt—for the first time in the six years I had known him.

"I think a clean lab coat would be in order." He smiled.

I found a white coat in a closet and, not sure how to wear it, buttoned it all the way to the top.

In the cafeteria, I picked up a tray, looked around, and suddenly understood the need for my attire: the students, residents, and fellows were all wearing white pants, white shirts, and white buck shoes. The nurses wore starched white uniforms and caps. Even the blue- and pink-clad candystripers looked snappy. The uniforms gave people an identifiable role.

I got to the head of the line, accepted a bowl of oily-brown liquid handed to me, and had my first encounter with oxtail soup. I've never determined the ingredients, but I believe they used the same oxtail for years to come.

A woman of military demeanour stood at the end of the rails beside the cash register, inspecting people's trays and greeting everyone as they passed.

Mrs. Cleghorn was her name and she obviously ruled the cafeteria and knew everyone.

"And who, may I ask, are you?" she said as I approached.

"My name is Phil Gold. I'll be working with Dr. Burgen on the twelfth floor."

"Oh," she said, clearly knowing everything, "you are in the University Medical Clinic."

How could I resist.

"Madam," I said, "I *am* the University Medical Clinic."

Mrs. Cleghorn and I became friends, both of us enjoying the banter with a laugh and a smile, and I was delighted when her brilliant son John went on to become president of the Royal Bank of Canada. She also began a habit of giving me extra desserts—and I've had trouble with my weight ever since.

I didn't know it, back in 1959, but my entire professional career would unfold on one floor or another of the new hospital. The circumstance reminds me of the song "Hotel California" by the Eagles and makes me chuckle: "You can check out any time you like / but you can never leave." Thankfully, my experience on Cedar Avenue was a bit more productive.

Married to Evelyn—and to Medicine

At the end of my third year of medical school, after Evelyn and I had dated for almost three years, it felt completely natural for me to ask her if she'd like to get married. Happily, she agreed.

Our wedding took place at the Chevra Kadisha B'Nai Jacob synagogue on Clanranald Avenue on August 21, 1960. Ev was twenty years old and I was almost twenty-four. Back then, women under twenty-one needed a parent's or guardian's approval to get married, so her father signed the marriage registry for her, with pleasure. Evelyn's maid of honour was her sister, Clara, and my best man was Mort Levy. Arnold was in England for the summer but came back early to attend our wedding, and my grade-one teacher, Esther Hoffman, surprised us by showing up at the chapel and giving us a kiss for good luck! For our honeymoon we drove down to the Catskills.

In September, I entered my last year of medical school. Meanwhile, Evelyn worked as a medical lab technician for Dr. Samuel Rabinovitch. Interestingly, his name is forever linked to Montreal's "Days of Shame," the antisemitic June 1934 doctors' strike at Notre Dame Hospital. For four days there, all of the interns and residents had walked off the job because Rabinovitch, a *Jew*, had been hired as a senior resident. Rabinovitch resigned to end the strike because he realized the danger to the patients.

Evelyn, who enjoyed business more than laboratory work, then changed jobs to work in the accounting department of Trans-Island Motors on Decarie Boulevard. She kept that job until Ian was born in 1962, at which point she took it upon herself to be a stay-at-home mother and wife *par excellence*.

ABOVE: Orange Julep, Decarie Boulevard, 1964, in its original concrete structure.

OPPOSITE TOP: Me, Evelyn, Malk, and Babbeh at Chevra Kadisha B'Nai Jacob Synagogue, August 21, 1960.

OPPOSITE BOTTOM: Our marriage ceremony under the chuppah.

But Evelyn did much more than that. Her volunteer work in many areas of the community continued, and she would become a critical volunteer in my office when later I took on the post of physician-in-chief. In many ways she got to know some of the staff and the residents better than I did, since she always had time to listen to anyone's problems. The significant ones were passed on at dinner.

And then there was her remarkable career as a pastel artist, in her "spare time." Her work was extraordinary, and went on to include weaving and tapestry in later decades.

Arnold had suggested I do two years of medical school. Instead, I found that medical school was both challenging and delightful. I completed all four years and received my MD degree. My lab work during the summers also produced good results and I completed an M.Sc. degree in physiology. By 1961, I believe that we had the purest preparation of erythropoietin in the world at the time. Mass production of erythropoietin, by recombinant DNA technology, was still a couple of decades away.

For me these were glorious, busy years.

On the last day of June, in 1961, which was a Friday, Evelyn finished typing up the thesis for my M.Sc. degree. I would start my rotating internship at the Montreal General the next week. I rushed to Arnold's office on the tenth floor and handed him my thesis. Over the next hour, as I sat watching him, he read it steadily in his usual fashion, wetting a finger as he turned the pages.

"Good first draft," he said.

"This is it," I replied. "I start my rotating internship on Monday."

He relented. At the fall convocation, I went up twice, once for my MD degree, and a second time for my M.Sc.

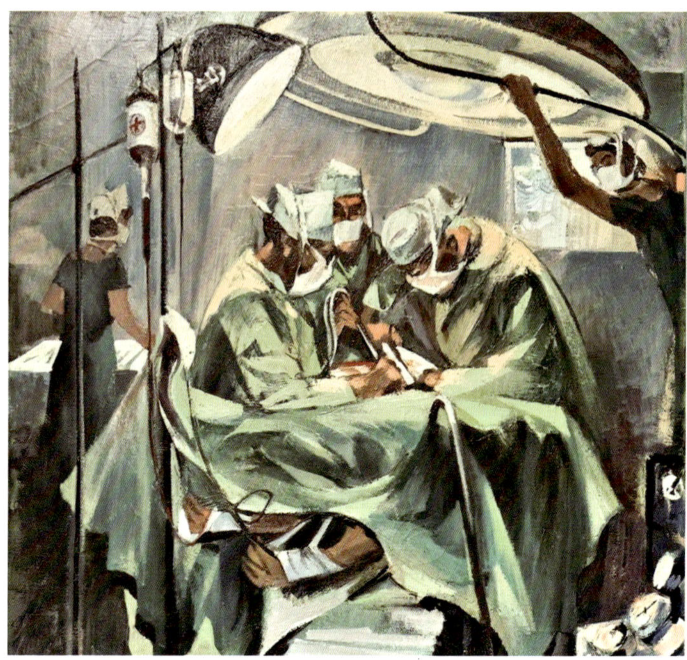

Albert Cloutier, OR *no. 10 — The Montreal General Hospital, featuring Drs. S.A. MacDonald, H. Rocke Robertson, and H.J. Scott*, 1961.

A Slice of Apple Pie

One Sunday morning at the Montreal General during my rotating internship, in the winter of 1961, a call came from Emergency requesting a surgeon. Both surgical residents were already in the operating rooms—leaving me, the intern, as the only doctor available.

I went to Emergency. The patient was a boy of eighteen who had come in with a bloody hand wrapped in a towel. Out hunting with his father, he had been clambering through a fence with the safety off, holding his rifle by the end of the muzzle like a walking stick, when it had discharged. The accident made a complete mess of his hand, but as I examined the site of his injury I could discern some bone structure and tendons still intact. This was good news. It meant he could probably keep the hand. I relayed the facts of the injury to his parents and told them I would get hold of Dr. W, our chief of plastic surgery, who had an international reputation for his superb work.

"No need," said the young man's father. He had already called Dr. A, an old friend, whom he trusted implicitly.

I tried not to flinch. Among medical staff and students, Dr. A was sometimes referred to as one of the Four Horsemen of the Apocalypse. But he had already been called, so the die was cast. Dr. A arrived, talked to the patient's father, then told me to scrub in for surgery.

Dr. H. Rocke Robertson: war surgeon, MGH Surgeon-in-Chief, Principal of McGill, Royal Society Fellow, and Companion of the Order of Canada.

"There's no one competent available," he said, "so you'd better try to assist me."

I entered the operating room (OR) as the patient was receiving an anesthetic and surgery was about to begin.

Dr. A examined the hand cursorily.

"Nope, nothing left," he pronounced. "There's nothing for it but amputation."

Taken aback, I pointed to the hand. "No, doctor, I can see some structure."

Dr. A turned on me angrily.

"How dare you?" he said, his eyes flaring above his surgical mask.

At that point I began to operate on autopilot. I removed my rubber gloves, a gesture that automatically stops all action in an OR, and turned to the nurses.

"Call Dr. W," I told one of the nurses.

She seemed confused. I repeated my request.

"Call Dr. W, before I go into the hall and scream for help."

She kept looking between Dr. A and me.

"Do it now!" I said, more firmly than I felt.

Dr. A scowled.

"You will never scrub with me again," he said.

"I'll take that as a promise," I replied and left the operating room.

I sat in the surgeons' lounge as, down the hall, Dr. A told Dr. W about the ill-mannered and insolent intern who should be removed from the training program immediately.

Dr. W came to the lounge and asked me what had happened. I told him the story without embellishment. He listened, then nodded.

"Well, we'd best go back in and finish the job," he said.

Back in OR, I had the pleasure of watching a superb surgeon at work. When I glanced up at the attending nurses, they smiled behind their masks.

I followed the patient's post-operative recovery. His hand looked somewhat the worse for wear, but it was functional. His parents had heard rumours about something happening during their son's surgery, so I told the three of them a slightly varnished story of the day, careful not to cast stones. Indeed, from that day onward, I felt a greater warmth among the hospital staff and my fellow trainees. Dr. A was not a popular figure, I learned. He and I never spoke again. He had, however, filed a complaint against me with the chair of surgery, Dr. H. Rocke Robertson. Dr. Robertson had spoken to a number of people involved in the events of that day. I was given a mild reprimand and a wink, and the matter was considered closed.

"Ah, Dr. Gold, you've been having a busy week," said Mrs. Cleghorn in the cafeteria the next day. "Wait a moment."

She reached under the counter and came up with a slice of apple pie.

"From the OR nurses," she said. "No charge, and don't change."

What's Your Specialty?

A major concern for graduates fresh out of medical school is choosing a specialty. This is no small decision, since it is a decision that will shape their entire professional life.

Some years ago, to help students struggling to choose theirs, I came up with the following formula:

1. *To cut or not to cut?* If you don't like the sight of blood, or making surgical incisions, or sewing up organs, then cutting is not for you. A huge swath of medical specialties is instantly ruled out when you make this visceral choice.

2. *Big people or little people?* No doctor enjoys seeing children in pain, but if this aspect of the job renders you dysfunctional, then you should avoid pediatrics and focus on big people instead.

If you don't like dealing with people, then radiology or pathology are options.

And if you'd rather help people with their psychological problems, welcome to psychiatry.

The completed Montreal General Hospital in the 1970s, still a state-of-the-art facility at the time.

My own experience may serve as an example. Partway through my rotating internship—the apprenticing year, no longer part of the curriculum, during which doctors tried out the different specialties available to them—I realized that surgery was not for me. "It's great fun," one surgeon said, "you'll love it." But despite the best efforts of surgical staff and residents to convince me otherwise, the truth is that I have ten thumbs and lack the precision required to be a surgeon. So, for me, cutting was out.

But when it came to the next question—big people or little people?—I couldn't decide.

Then I did a stint at the Montreal Children's Hospital in April 1962. There I met a boy of about eleven years old on the wards. He had been admitted to hospital many times for congenital biliary atresia, a condition where malformed ducts impede bile from exiting the liver properly, leading to severe jaundice and liver damage. Diagnosis is usually made shortly after birth. My young friend had lived with an enlarged liver and spleen his entire life.

His skin and the whites of his eyes were a dark yellow-green. He'd been on the ward often and knew the staff and their schedules. When he was feeling well enough, he spent his time talking with his fellow young patients who weren't as familiar with hospitals as he was, helping them acclimatize to the strange environment.

I got to know him quite well. We talked about what it was like being readmitted to hospital so often. He felt bad for his parents, who worried about him constantly. He hoped to become a doctor one day so he could help other sick people.

After the early weeks of my rotation—two weeks of dayshifts, with frequent nightshifts—I finally had a weekend off. I was delighted. Our first child, Ian, had just been born and I was desperate to get home to see him and my wife. We had a lovely weekend and I returned to the hospital refreshed on Monday, ready to go. And that's when I learned my jaundiced young friend had died over the weekend.

I'm still not quite sure of what happened to me that day. I believe I remained competent and functional, and continued my daily ward activities. But at some point over the next forty-eight hours I started to feel that if I left the hospital, another child would die.

Friday morning the attending pediatrician on the ward, Clifford Golden, asked me to meet him in the cafeteria. After some small talk and a coffee, he asked:

"What is it like to be God?"

"I wouldn't know. Why would you ask?" I said.

"Well, Phil, I've heard from the nurses that you think you're God," he said.

"What do you mean?" I asked.

"Apparently you think that if you go home, another patient will die."

I thought for a moment. Hearing Clifford Golden say those words made me realize the weirdness of my thinking.

"Is it that bad?" I asked.

"Yes, it is," he said. "Now go home."

I did as I was told and crossed pediatrics off my list of possible specialties.

I don't recall doing a psychiatry rotation in my internship, but an earlier exposure to the field during my fourth year of medical school is indelible.

A small group of students, including me, were gathered in Verdun at what is now the Douglas Mental Health University Institute. Our instructor, whose name I've blotted from my memory, showed us two patients. The first, he said, suffered from schizophrenia and was a notable fabricator of neologisms, that is, words she made up. As we arrived outside the locked door of her small room (this was before deconfinement; patients are no longer treated this way), she began to bang on the door and shout, "*Laz mikh aroys, laz mikh aroys, laz mikh aroys.*"

"Note her use of nonsense words," our instructor said.

"I have no doubt that she's schizophrenic," I spoke up, "but what she's saying in Yiddish is *Let me out*. Can't blame her for that."

"Oh, really?" our instructor replied blithely.

The next patient he showed us was a mentally challenged woman with a rather small head. One of the manifestations of her condition, he emphasized, was an inability to abstract. To demonstrate this, he presented her with an orange and a banana, named them, and asked if she knew what they were.

"I have juice from the orange every morning," she replied, "but I don't know what is a bannnnana."

"So what do the orange and the banana have in common?" he asked her.

"I told you I don't know what is a bannnnana, but an orange is a fruit."

The instructor seemed unimpressed by her answer.

Strike psychiatry, perhaps unfairly, from my choices.

A Fibrillation Tale

Not too long ago, a heart attack was frequently a death sentence. In the 1950s and '60s, Paul Zoll had performed cutting-edge cardiac resuscitation using alternating current shocks through the chest wall. Bernard Lown subsequently helped to develop today's standard direct-current defibrillators with capacitors that hold a steady charge.

But such techniques were not generally known when I was a young physician. Prior to the event described below, I had seen only a short training film on external cardiac massage, read some medical literature on the subject, and noted a newspaper report about some firefighters in Baltimore who had resuscitated a person who'd suffered a cardiac arrest.

In spring 1963, I was the in-house medical resident at the Queen Mary Veterans Hospital, before it was converted to a chronic-care residence. It had been a relatively quiet day and I was doing some reading.

Around dinnertime, I received a call from one of the head nurses to "come and pronounce a patient dead." I quickly went to the ward and, looking at the patient, told the nurse that I might have trouble pronouncing him dead

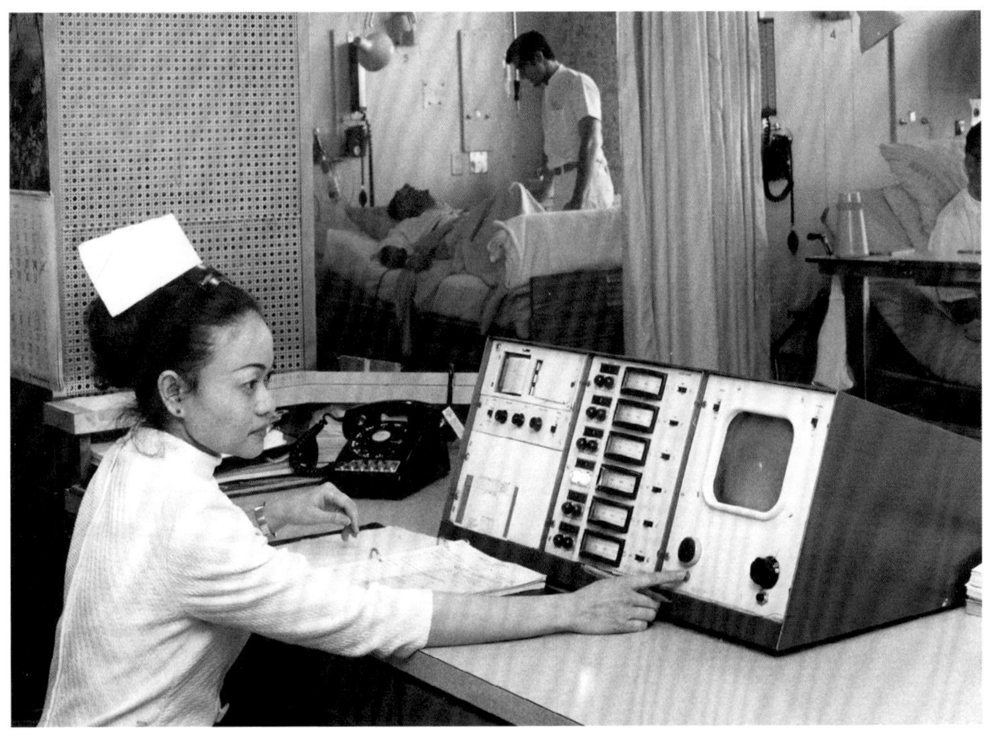

The General's new Cardiac Monitoring Unit circa 1970.

since he was still gasping for air. But I could get no pulse and his pupils were beginning to dilate. As we wheeled him into the hall, I initiated cardiac massage and mouth-to-mouth resuscitation. The nurse cautioned me to be quiet since some of the other patients were snoozing.

Too focused to be surprised, I told the nurse to call the cardiac arrest team.

She went quickly down the hall about twenty-five yards before turning back. "What's a cardiac arrest team?" she asked.

"Call an orderly," I told her. "Ask him to bring an EKG machine, an electrical wire cut off a lamp, and some aluminum foil if he can find it."

And then I set into chest compressions.

As I pumped rhythmically, I remembered that Bernard Lown had used direct current, and I only had alternating current. But it seemed to me that beggars could not be choosers: the patient had severe obstructive pulmonary disease and a very stiff chest wall. Thankfully I soon felt the chest wall give and the massage became much easier.

We'll deal with the chest trauma later, I thought.

After a few minutes, a bright young orderly named Johnny appeared with my list of items. He adeptly hooked up the EKG apparatus, which showed the patient was in ventricular fibrillation.

"Okay, separate the positive and negative wires of the electric cord," I told him, "then strip the ends of the wires and wrap them in aluminum foil."

Johnny did as I asked.

"All right, now flatten out the ends of the foil."

By this time the nurse had actually taken some initiative and called an anesthesiologist, who was now quietly and unobtrusively intubating the patient and maintaining good ventilation.

The time had come. I attached one of the wires just to the left of the upper sternum, and the other in the mid-clavicular line of the fifth left intercostal space, so the contacts spread across the heart. I then made sure my hands were clear of the area and asked the orderly to insert the plug into the electrical outlet for two seconds. He did so.

The corridor lights dimmed. I could see the jolting contraction of the patient's chest musculature and smell the charring skin. The EKG showed a short, flat line—then the ventricular fibrillation continued. After a few more chest compressions, I relocated my makeshift electrodes slightly and asked for another two-second burst.

To my great surprise and delight, the audible sizzle of electric current was followed by a few strange squiggles on the EKG, and then a normal EKG pattern appeared on the monitor. Within a few minutes the patient opened his eyes. Remarkably, his pupils appeared quite normal and reacted to light. After removing the endotracheal tube, the patient was also able to breath on his own. To no one's surprise, he complained of pain on both sides of his detached sternum and where I had toasted his skin.

We moved him gingerly onto a gurney and I called Harvey Sigman, chief surgical resident, who had made the cardiac training film available. Harvey expertly stabilized the patient's chest in the operating room. Later, over coffee, he asked me what kind of a day I'd had. Despite that question, we still remain friendly.

The next morning, on rounds, I recounted the adventures of the previous evening to my fellow physicians, nurses, and the patient. Everyone appeared impressed except the patient himself, who was a World War II veteran. As I was leaving the room, he tugged at my sleeve.

"Am I 100 percent pensionable now?" he asked.

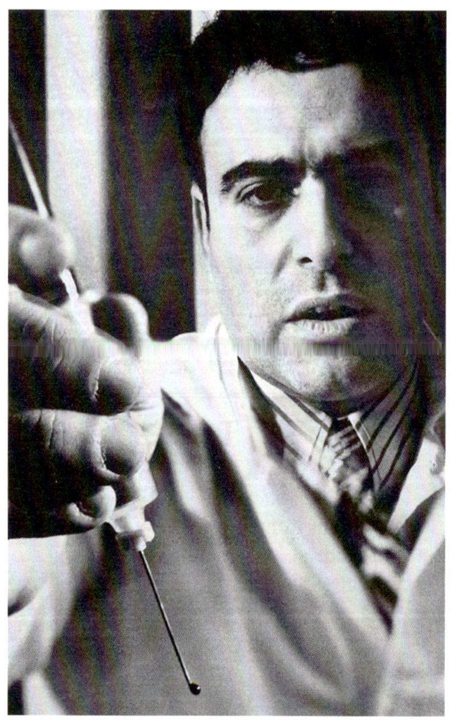

LIFE
BUSY REBEL
Jane Fonda, Pusher of Causes
A Breakthrough Cancer Test
APRIL 23 • 1971 • 50¢

PART III

Toward CEA

Immunological Tolerance

After my rotating internship year, I began a year of residency at the Montreal General in internal medicine, a wide-ranging area of medicine that runs the gamut of human illnesses that don't fall under surgery or psychiatry.

As I walked the wards, I couldn't help but notice the great number of cancer patients. Oncology, the study and treatment of tumours, had not yet become a specialty with its own units and beds. Many patients on the wards had had their tumours removed surgically and virtually all of them were receiving chemotherapy and/or radiation, regardless of the type of tumour involved. It's no exaggeration to say treatment for cancer back then was two parts pragmatic, one part science—and a lot of hope.

That approach didn't appeal to me. Too many people were suffering, and the problem was starting to keep me up at night. The major questions that bothered me were: What made cancer cells different from normal cells? Was there nothing specific we could define in the cancer cell? At that time, after a century of research, no tumour-specific molecules had been identified that I could find in the medical literature. And there was a good reason for this. How do you isolate and identify molecules, from a single type of cancer, among the tens of millions of molecules that make up a human cell? And then the thought occurred to me: if you're searching for a needle in the haystack, first remove the haystack.

But how?

Around that time, I attended a Grand Round lecture on the phenomenon of "immunological tolerance" given by Montreal physician Bram Rose. Rose was one of the first immunologists to work at McGill, and the research he discussed in his lecture, carried out by Sir Peter Medawar and his colleagues in Britain, suggested to me a possible path forward. I began to consider how the use of immunologic tolerance might be applied to the search for the tumour-specific components of the cancer cell.

OPPOSITE TOP: Residency staff of the Montreal General, 1962. I am sitting cross-legged in front of the two administrators in grey suits.

OPPOSITE BOTTOM LEFT: From *Life* magazine, April 23, 1971. I am testing a blood sample.

OPPOSITE BOTTOM RIGHT: Jane Fonda on the cover of that issue, with "A Breakthrough Cancer Test" as the second headline. Beauty before antigens!

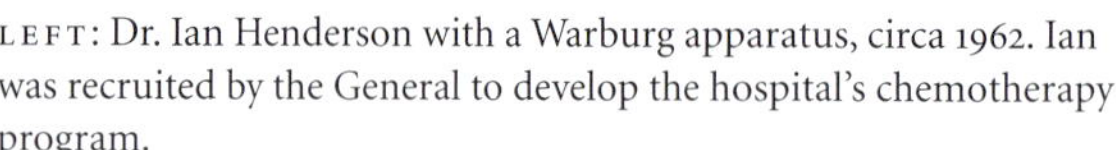

LEFT: Dr. Ian Henderson with a Warburg apparatus, circa 1962. Ian was recruited by the General to develop the hospital's chemotherapy program.

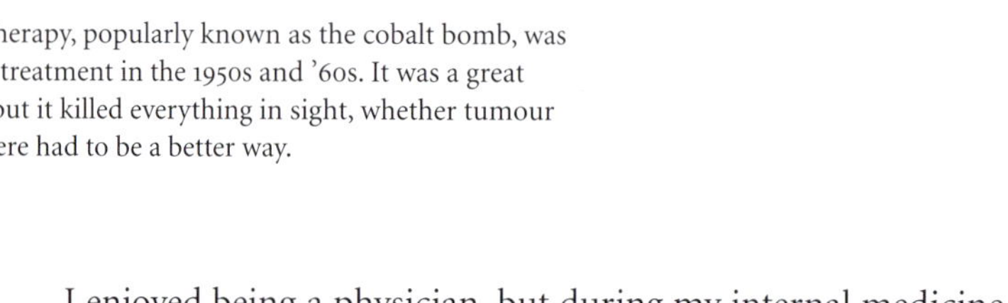

RIGHT: Cobalt-60 therapy, popularly known as the cobalt bomb, was a standard radiation treatment in the 1950s and '60s. It was a great advance at the time but it killed everything in sight, whether tumour or normal tissue. There had to be a better way.

I enjoyed being a physician, but during my internal medicine residency I began to realize that if I wanted to find better ways to treat cancer, the problem would need a great deal of research, and even more luck.

I raised the prospect of pursuing cancer immunology with Arnold Burgen.

"It's an interesting thought," he said, "but the field of cancer research is littered with the bodies of researchers with interesting thoughts."

He said I'd do better to keep studying erythropoietin.

As I've written, Arnold was the only true genius I've ever met, and his experience and insight were beyond reproach, yet I must admit I scratched my head at his response.

But then, after thirteen years at McGill, Arnold announced he would be returning to his native country to assume one of the most prestigious positions in academic science: he would be Sheild Professor of Pharmacology at Cambridge University, starting in the fall of 1962. Arnold's star continued to rise in the 1970s when he became director of the National Institute for Medical Research at Mill Hill, and his impact on medicine and science earned him a knighthood.

Sir Arnold influenced my life and career greatly. But his move to Cambridge may have been fortuitous for me: he was strongly against choosing cancer research as a future career.

Before Arnold left Montreal, I went to see him in the University Medical Clinic to say my farewell. On the wall behind him in his office was an old black-and-white picture of what appeared to be a rabbi.

"You've seen this picture, haven't you?" Arnold asked me.

I nodded.

"Have you ever wanted to ask me about it?"

I knew Arnold was Jewish, but he was a gentleman of an older generation, one that did not make a point of "showing one's Jewishness," as he put it. Our relationship was based on science. In the nearly ten years we had known each other, we had never discussed our shared ethnicity or religion.

"This is my grandfather. I'm embarrassed to say I've never taken great pride in my heritage. But you do and I'm glad that you do."

Arnold and I have remained good friends to this day. As I write, he is ninety-nine years old, the founding president of Academia Europaea, whip-smart as ever. His wife, the brilliant crystallographer Olga Kennard, is ninety-seven.

Toward CEA

Knowing that Arnold would be leaving Montreal, I approached Sam Freedman, director of the Division of Allergy, with the idea of using immunologic technology to try to identify markers of malignant tumours. I had to sell the idea to someone who had lab space, access to a bit of funding for materials, and an interest in immunology.

"Sam, if you have any sense at all, you'll tell me to bugger off," I said jokingly.

To my surprise and delight, he thought the effort was worth a try. He offered me $5,000 of research funding for materials for the year, a good piece of bench space, used lab equipment that could be revamped, and access to an animal facility. And so after one year of medical residency, I left the wards of the General and moved back into the laboratories of the McGill University Medical Clinic (UMC), which was now located on the tenth floor of the General.

The UMC was an extraordinary place. People who worked there included Charlie Hollenberg, John Krupey, Ron Hopkirk, Carl Goresky, and other outstanding scientists whom I would get to know better with time. John Krupey, the best intuitive chemist I've ever met, would join me in what later became known as the Carcinoembryonic Antigen (CEA) Research Group. My days with erythropoietin were over. I would now be chasing the white rabbit down the hole, in search of cancer molecules.

Carl Goresky in his laboratory at the Montreal General Hospital Research Institute, 1976. Carl's pioneering work on how the human liver functions made him a world-class researcher in the areas of transmembrane transport and intracellular metabolism.

I spent the next two years in the lab, doing research that ultimately led to my Ph.D. in physiology but, more importantly, identified the marker of the bowel cancer cell. I would return to study that molecule for many years to come.

My initial research idea was quite simple, as I've said: if you're looking for a needle in a haystack, first remove the haystack.

In more scientific terms, here's how it worked:

The thymus gland is a most remarkable organ. It sits in the top part of the chest just behind the breastbone and between the lungs. When all mammals are in their mother's uterus, and perhaps for a short while after birth, the thymus gland produces lymphocytes, immunity-controlling cells that, by a remarkable random association of molecular fragments, learn how to mount an immune response to hundreds of millions, or even billions, of foreign antigenic molecules. It is then the *second* job of the thymus to destroy any cell with the ability to react against "self," a sort of clearing of the deck, which prepares the immune system to identify and react to *foreign* molecular structures—bacterial, viral, or any other invading organism. Foreign tissue grafts are likewise rejected.

Me, seated, with a summer resident, Michael. God knows what either of us is doing—I barely recognize the lab apparatus in this photo. High tech in the 1940s meant a ballpoint pen and a calculator with four functions. In my lifetime, the half-life of scientific knowledge (the time it takes for half of what we believe to be replaced by new information) has gone from about fifty years to under ten. Soon it may be measured in months. Any great-grandchildren of mine reading this may wonder how people got along without robots or artificial intelligence, or why it took hours to fly across continents instead of minutes.

Why then, if certain cells become cancerous, doesn't the body reject them? Perhaps the immune system tries and fails to identify malignant cells. Could an "immunologic mechanism of searching" turn up the elusive cancer molecule produced by the malignant cell?

Such theories could not be studied easily in humans. But the work of Sir Peter Medawar, described by Bram Rose in his lecture, suggested a way forward. In 1953, the Nobel Prize–winning biologist Sir Peter Medawar and his colleagues showed that if they exposed mouse A, at or before birth, to the cells of another strain of mouse (mouse B), then mouse A would not react against the tissue of mouse B later in life, as would normally be the case. Medawar had demonstrated "acquired immunologic tolerance." Mouse A now identified the cells of mouse B as self.

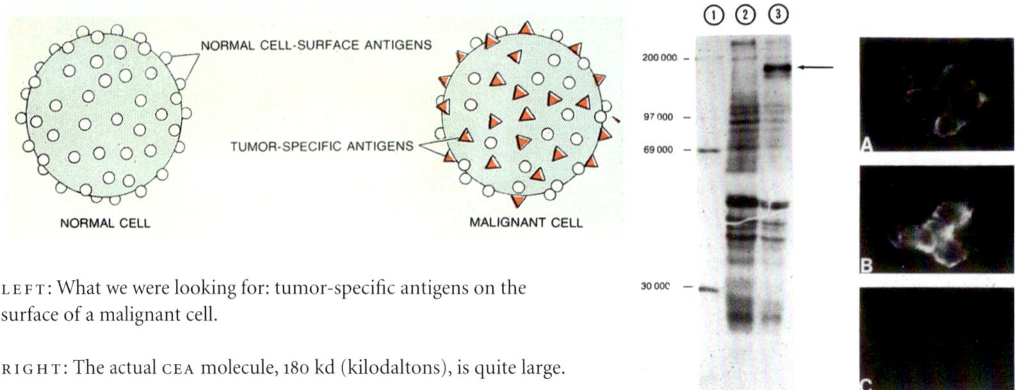

LEFT: What we were looking for: tumor-specific antigens on the surface of a malignant cell.

RIGHT: The actual CEA molecule, 180 kd (kilodaltons), is quite large.

FAR RIGHT: The real thing: electron-microscopy image of CEA on the surface of a cell, illuminated by fluorescein.

Through Arnold, I got in touch with Sir Peter and asked him if he had ever tested his theories of tolerance *between* species.

"No, I haven't," he said, "but good luck to you, and let me know how it goes." I would.

To find the elusive cancer molecule, I worked between humans and rabbits. With the consent of colon cancer patients at the General, the enormous help of the hospital's surgeons and operating room nurses, and the cooperation of the terrific pathologist-in-chief, Dr. William Duguid, I was able to acquire and extract both normal and cancerous tissues from the bowels of patients undergoing attempted curative surgery. (I used bowel cancer because, the way the cancer grows, it's possible to obtain normal and cancerous tissue from the same patients during a single surgery.)

To establish the proverbial haystack, I transferred into newborn rabbits an extract from the *normal bowel tissue* and then, later, once the newborn rabbits had hopefully acquired immunologic tolerance to the healthy tissue, I injected the same rabbits with the unhealthy or tumorous tissue from the *same patient*, to see if the cancer-specific molecule (the needle) would show itself.

One difficulty with my experiment was that mother rabbits do not like their offspring to be handled by strangers: the foreign smell of a human leads the mothers to kill their offspring immediately. To overcome this, I had to spend a few hours a day for a couple of months at a time with pregnant rabbits in the animal rooms of the UMC, until they recognized my smell and wouldn't kill their offspring. I was a fully trained physician working towards his Ph.D., but to most people in the hospital I was the guy who looked after (and distinctly smelled like) the rabbits. I often had coffee alone.

Once the mothers trusted me with their offspring, I injected their newborns within eight hours of their birth with the normal colon tissue of a cancer patient. I did not know at this stage whether the rabbits would develop immunologic tolerance or not. But if all went well, their immune systems would soon treat the normal tissue as "self" and not a foreign agent. This would remove the "haystack" of normal molecules from the experiment.

Some three months later, I injected the same rabbits with cancerous bowel tissue from the same patients. This was the needle in the haystack I was looking for. Would the rabbits' immune systems be able to differentiate the cells, and identify the hoped-for, tumour-specific molecule?

In September 1963, to finally test the outcome, I set up the gel plates (my method of analysis at the time) on a Friday afternoon and brought them home to assess the next day. I stashed them in a high cupboard, where our young son Ian couldn't get at them. And the next morning, after coffee with Ev, we took a look at the plates.

There it was: a single, white band in the gel plate. We had found it, the "marker" that had been sought for over a century. The baby rabbits' immune systems had treated the normal tissue as self and the tumour-specific molecule as foreign. For the first time in medical science, using a rabbit's immune system, we had found a way to identify, and later isolate and analyze, the tumour-specific molecule of the human digestive system. We would later identify the same molecule in embryonic human bowel tissue in the first six months of pregnancy; hence, I named the tumour-specific molecule carcinoembryonic antigen, or CEA.

That weekend, I achieved a goal I had imagined twenty years earlier in the library at Bancroft Elementary: to know something that no one else on the planet knew. Colon cancer had a specific component not present in the corresponding normal tissue. That component was CEA, and I had found it.

On Monday, I walked around the corridors of the Montreal General, basically telling any colleague who would listen what I had found.

Sam Freedman and I published these initial results in the *Journal of Experimental Medicine* in 1965. This ultimately led to CEA being the first molecule sanctioned as a tumour marker by the Food and Drug Administration (FDA) in the United States, and then by all such agencies internationally.

The next phase of the work was to determine if and when CEA could be detected in the blood of patients. We knew that the concentrations would be miniscule, and the only rational approach would be to establish a radioimmunoassay (RIA) for CEA, using cutting-edge developments in the application of radioactive iodine. These would be the kind of studies that Rosalyn Yalow had done for insulin and for which she would win the Nobel Prize in 1977. During this phase, I was happy to have the help of Dr. David Hawkins, with whom I'd worked during my residency at the Montreal General and who had done RIA work at the Scripps Clinic in La Jolla, California.

We found that we could detect a billionth of a gram of CEA in a millilitre of blood. We then went on to show the presence of CEA in various increased

What $300,000 could get you in the 1970s: the new MGH Research Institute takes shape.

concentrations in the blood of bowel cancer patients at different points in their disease. We published these studies in 1967. Use of the RIA for CEA subsequently became the standard test for diagnosis, prognosis, and recurrence of bowel cancer. Indeed, it became the standard of care.

In the mid-1970s, the pharmaceutical giant Hoffmann-La Roche (Roche) became interested in our work and, after several meetings, offered to buy the CEA assay for commercialization. Since our funding came from the Medical Research Council of Canada and the National Cancer Institute of Canada, we asked them for their blessing to pursue the sale. They wanted no part of the discussion. When McGill University said much the same thing, I left it to the hospital's legal team to negotiate the sale. The hospital received $300,000 from Roche for the test, a major assist to the construction of the MGH Research Institute, next door to the hospital. But no one, and certainly not I, thought to ask for royalties on future sales. This is rather unfortunate since worldwide sales of the CEA assay topped $2 billion annually in 2019 alone. Oh well, upward and onward.

Over the next several years, the presence of carcinoembryonic antigen was demonstrated in some 70 percent of all human cancers, regardless of origin, in our laboratory and others. The genetics of CEA and its related series of family members was defined in a number of laboratories, and most particularly at the Goodman Cancer Research Centre, by a number of superb scientists, including Abe Fuks, Cliff Stanners, and Nicole Beauchemin. Nicole defined the series of molecules she named the CEACAM (CEA cell adhesion molecules), as they are known internationally.

As the work on CEA mushroomed locally, nationally, and around the world, the next decade became a wild ride, with a variety of tumour markers found in other laboratories. These included prostate-specific antigen (PSA), alpha-fetoprotein (AFP), Ca19-9, and on and on. Many of the investigators involved spent time in our laboratory. Interestingly, some fifty-five years later, CEA is still the tumour marker most often used in clinical medicine.

I met Sir Peter Medawar at a conference some years after our first talk. "I'll tell you," he said to me, "I didn't think it would work."

I told Sir Peter there were times I also had doubts, and that I felt incredibly fortunate in the way CEA and its progenitors have developed.

The biomedical adventure that began so long ago has continued for over half a century. But from those early, intense years working with CEA, I learned that of the three things that determine one's life—genes, environment, and luck—if you have a choice, take luck.

Just One More Year

By 1965, if I had wanted, I could have become a GP (general practitioner of medicine) in relatively short order. But my investigation of CEA and immunologic tolerance had barely scratched the surface, so I wasn't going to give that up. Yet at the same time, my passion for seeing patients remained strong. So I decided to continue my specialty training as a physician alongside my research activities. The balance was possible, really, because my laboratory was only a few hundred yards away from the wards in the same complex, and because I had trusted colleagues like John Krupey to run the lab. Achieving one's research goals can take years, whereas success with patients often occurs relatively quickly. I really enjoyed being on the wards. Seeing patients improve is a delight and an aspect of my career that I cherish greatly.

For Ev and me, as a couple, every step I took in the ensuing decade became "just one more year." After my rotating internship (1961–62) in which I trained at various hospitals in Montreal, I did a year of residency at the General in internal medicine (1962–63), then "just two more years" at the University Medical Clinic, housed in the General, to achieve my Ph.D. in physiology (1963–65). Then "just one more year" of residency (1965–66), again at the General, in internal medicine, and after passing the internal medicine exams of the Royal College of Physicians, in 1966, I chose clinical immunology and allergy as my specialty. It only made sense, since much of

Expo 67 in Montreal. The summer before we left for New York, I consulted on the creation of the Man and His Health pavilion at the fair. Miracles in Modern Medicine, an experimental film by Robert Cordier that played in the pavilion's Meditheatre, shocked many visitors with its closeups of surgical interventions, nuclear medicine, and portraits of suffering patients in Montreal hospitals. The point was not to shock, of course, but to inform the public of advances in medical and surgical care.

my work on CEA had involved the use of immunologic technology. Then "just one more year" (1966–67) on an allergy-immunology fellowship with Sam Freedman, also at the General. Over these years, while continuing my research in the lab, I saw patients suffering from allergy- and immunology-related ailments on the wards and in the allergy clinic. Dr. Howard Mitchell, former director of the Allergy division, who retired when Sam Freedman took on the directorship, was kind enough to let me have his office on the seventh floor of the hospital.

Ev took all this in stride until the summer of 1967 when I announced that "just one more year" of postdoctoral training would take us, that fall, to the Public Health Research Institute in New York. She protested the idea quite strongly. By that time, we had two toddlers, Ian and Josie (Joel hadn't arrived yet), and we were happily settled at 5705 Parkhaven Avenue in Côte St-Luc, a short drive from Ev's parents' house. Family was the foundation of Evelyn's life and the early years of our marriage showed me she was the consummate mother. Relocating to New York would take us away from family—no small

The bright lights of the Big Apple: midtown Manhattan in 1968. We loved our year abroad. Over my shoulder Ev is saying, "I couldn't wait to get back home." Oh well!

matter. Ev finally recalled her mother's saying, "*Mit a Mann, über dem yam.*" ("With your husband, over the ocean.") And so we decided to do it.

Over that year I had a good learning experience in the lab of Dr. Sam Dales at the New York Public Health Research Laboratories, where with the help of a terrific technician, Harriet Silverberg, I learned the procedures of electron microscopy, virology, and tissue-culture technology, all things that I badly needed to develop my work back in Montreal. I kept my lab going at the UMC through frequent telephone conversations with staff and students, and periodic visits. Meanwhile, during evenings and weekends in the Big Apple, Ev and I enjoyed theatre on Broadway, music and dance at Lincoln Center, and wandering around the city to our heart's content with Ian and Josie. Our son Joel is now a psychiatrist working in Manhattan. It took him a long while to receive his green card and American citizenship. He says half-jokingly, "You left New York too soon!"

In 1968, our "just one more year" phase finally came to an end and we returned to our home on Parkhaven, where we lived for the next twenty years or so while I worked at the Montreal General and McGill. When all three of our children were old enough to attend grade school, Ev turned to her talent for graphic art, shifting from pastel painting into weaving and other art forms. Ev has often thought of what she might have accomplished had she stayed in the working world. But she feels her greatest accomplishment was raising our children to be terrific people.

Back in Montreal, I set up a routine where I passed Tuesday mornings with patients in the allergy clinic and spent the rest of the week in the lab on the tenth floor of the General. While I was away, Sam Freedman had told me about two excellent young staff he was recruiting: David Hawkins and Joseph Shuster. I already knew David from his help with the CEA radioimmunoassay. He went on to an outstanding career in clinical rheumatology and research, and was appointed dean of the Faculty of Medicine of Memorial University in 1987. He served in many high-profile academic posts in Canada, the United States, and abroad. David died, far too young, in 2011.

Joe Shuster was a passing acquaintance of mine from high school, where he was a year behind me at Baron Byng. But he became a great friend and colleague, and we worked together for the next fifty years—our entire clinical careers. Joe has the remarkable capacity of remaining calm during almost any situation. Since I passed his home on my morning drive to work, for the next seventeen years I regularly picked him up on the way to the hospital and often dropped him off again in the evening. This gave us time to discuss the matters of the day, medical, research-related, and anything else that came to mind. He was always available to help and became a mainstay in every aspect of my work at the Research Institute and in the hospital. He had such a good effect on me that Evelyn often referred to him as my "sedative." Joe had a brilliant career in Clinical Immunology and Allergy, chairing the division for some twenty-five years, during which he was also the director of the Research Institute.

Our work on CEA continued uninterrupted into the 1970s, with good success. National and international colleagues would come by quite regularly. For example, Dr. Anthony Fauci, who back then was a clinical associate at the National Institute of Allergy and Infectious Diseases (NIAID), would come by once a year to see how the CEA studies were going. Fauci has, of course, become a household name during the COVID-19 pandemic, no thanks to Donald Trump.

Over the years I received many offers to move my research activities to various high-profile university research centres in Boston, Paris, London, and elsewhere, but I realized I could accomplish what I wanted to do with less angst at the Montreal General and at McGill. It's a decision I've never regretted.

The cigarette: the deadliest artifact in the history of human civilization. In the 1960s I was smoking three packs a day. The prospect of hurting my family through second-hand smoke finally broke my habit.

BOTTOM RIGHT: Still from William Talman's anti-smoking commercial for the American Cancer Society, 1968. By the time it aired, Talman was already dead.

How I Quit Smoking

It seems absolutely astonishing today, but throughout the 1960s, even as I sought to identify a marker for cancer, I was a smoker.

I started smoking in late August 1958, during a week spent alone in the Laurentians preparing for my second year of medical school. I was at IT-L-DO, the cottage owned by Joe and Chana Katz, my future in-laws. Evelyn offered me a cigarette. She wasn't much of a smoker, but she had the occasional one. I had never smoked, but my first cigarette was a Craven A: I remember the distinctive red-and-white packaging. I can't recall what I enjoyed about the next few minutes, but on Monday morning, after everyone had left, I made my way to the corner store to buy my first package of cigarettes. By the time the family returned on Friday, I had made my way through my first-year pathology notes, along with a dozen cigarettes each day. My habit grew to three packs a day over the next dozen years.

Back then, the relationship between smoking and lung cancer was not yet well established. Smoking was part of the culture: in films, in magazine ads, on talk shows, on book covers. At the General during morning rounds, there was always an ashtray on the chart carrier (though we never smoked in patient rooms), and people routinely smoked in the lab as they worked. If you go up to the tenth floor of the Montreal General today, you might still be able to see the burns from cigarettes I left on the edges of tables in my lab.

When definitive studies of smoking and lung cancer were done in both animals and humans, the facts were incontrovertible: cigarettes are the deadliest artifact in the history of human civilization. Unfortunately, tobacco-industry propaganda covered up and compromised public awareness of this knowledge for decades, keeping millions of people like me smoking. Indeed, when we lived on Parkhaven, I would often go out on snowy evenings to pick up cigarettes from a small strip mall a few blocks away.

As suspicion about cigarettes and lung cancer grew during the 1960s, I started to worry but kept on smoking. After Josie was born in 1965, Evelyn asked me when there would be enough evidence to convince me that smoking could be lethal for me—and that second-hand smoke could be damaging our children's lungs. I agreed, kept worrying, and kept on smoking.

OPPOSITE TOP LEFT: Sir Peter Medawar, National Portrait Gallery, London.

TOP RIGHT: Sir Arnold Burgen, after his appointment as director of the National Institute for Medical Research in England, 1976.

BOTTOM: Joe Shuster and me, Montreal General Hospital.

During those years I became chair of the committee evaluating research grants for the American Cancer Society. In summer 1968 in New York City, at its offices where we routinely gathered, I was asked if I wanted to meet the famous actor William Talman, who played D.A. Hamilton Burger on the legal-drama TV series *Perry Mason*. To be polite, I went into the other suite where he was the centre of attention. Introductions were made, we chatted for a few minutes, and then I went back to my grants committee meeting without really inquiring as to why he was there.

Some months later, watching television in Montreal, I saw Talman's face on the screen. He was making a public service announcement about smoking and cancer from his home in California. After presenting his wife and children, the camera cut to Talman himself: "You know, I didn't really mind losing those courtroom battles. But I'm in a battle right now that I don't want to lose at all, because if I lose it, it means losing my wife and those kids you've just met. I've got lung cancer. So take some advice about smoking and losing from someone who's been doing both for years. If you don't smoke, don't start. If you do smoke, quit. Don't be a loser."

Talman was already dead. He had died of lung cancer on August 30, 1968, a few weeks after we met in New York.

That was it for me. My son Joel had just been born, and something had to give. I tossed my last package of cigarettes across the room, the way Cyrano de Bergerac tossed away his purse containing all the gold he owned, saying, "Ah, but the moment." In my mind, it was my final adieu to smoking. And I couldn't renege.

Evelyn and I have lived a smoke-free life ever since. Thanks to William Talman, the unbearable thought of hurting my family saved my life.

Meropi V.

Phil and Evelyn Gold, wedding dance, August 21, 1960.

PART IV

Dear Children

Becoming a Family Man

During the 1960s and 1970s, I travelled quite a lot for work. As a member of many professional societies, I regularly attended conferences across Canada and around the globe. And when I was back home in Montreal, there was the lab to run and endless hospital and university responsibilities. I had vowed to be as good a father and husband as I possibly could, but getting the balance right was sometimes a challenge.

I remember one Friday afternoon, returning from yet another trip abroad, to find Ev and the children sitting on the front porch. As I got out of the taxi, Ev pointed to me.

"Children, you see that man?" she said. "He's your father. Now go and say, *Hi, Daddy*."

Thankfully, there weren't many moments like this, and that wasn't the father I became. Quite the opposite: I made it to every hockey and basketball game the boys ever played. At the rink, I became the guy who calmed down the other fathers after a bad call, or separated angry parents before a brawl started.

For Josie, I held one end of the skipping rope, with the other tied to the garage door, and became the "ever-ender," as she called me. I also made it to all her ballet recitals and took her to all her rehearsals.

Watching the boys at sports and Josie at ballet were great experiences for me. I had not been very athletic as a boy. I knew how to swim, played baseball and football on Fletcher's Field and water polo for Baron Byng. But my hand-eye coordination and sense of balance were mediocre.

When I became a father, one memory from childhood kept bubbling up in me. It involved my father's failure to teach me how to ride a bicycle. He tried only once, in the early 1940s, one summer in the Laurentian village of

Evelyn Gold, *The Golden Years*, our front door at 5705 Parkhaven Avenue in Côte St-Luc.

ABOVE: The family in the mid-1970s in Trout Lake, before our trip to Israel: Joel, Ian, me, Josie, and Ev.

Lesage. He took me to a rocky field of scrub grass and uneven surfaces, with a borrowed adult-sized bike. Then he held the seat as I got on, gave me a great push, and shouted, "*Pedal! Pedal!*"

I fell off almost immediately. We tried again: same result. The field was too rocky to gain any momentum, and it seemed to me that I was miles off the ground. Another try, another fall. My father was not a natural teacher. Riding a bike was self-explanatory to him: you just did it. And if you couldn't, that was your problem.

No surprise, then, that after some five minutes he grew frustrated and impatient, and left me in the field. He never tried to teach me to ride again. But twenty years later, could I still be angry about it and still be blaming him? Such thoughts would occasionally run through my mind as I stood in cold arenas, watching my boys compete beautifully and grow into themselves. Rationally, I knew that if I had *really* wanted to ride a bike, I would have found a way. But I hadn't gone near a bike for years—in fact, it was the prospect of teaching my own children that had dredged up the old memory. So why was I still blaming my father? Was he really to blame, or was I simply holding on to an old feeling of distress?

I realized there was no "cure" for such feelings, but in St. Richard's churchyard in Côte St-Luc, near our home on Parkhaven Avenue, I taught Ian, Josie, and Joel how to ride a bike. Doing so gave them childhoods closer to that one I wished I'd had, created some kind of vicarious second chance, for me, and wrapped a layer of happiness around the memory.

And in the process, I developed a new empathy for my father. He had been so busy putting bread on the table for us, he had missed out on the joys of fatherhood. I loved him as, I believe, he loved me in his own way, but the stresses of his life, the loss of his entire family in the Holocaust, and his crushed political ideals had locked him inside himself. And the key was gone, or at least lost.

In 2020, Evelyn and I celebrated our sixtieth anniversary. We've had a wonderful marriage. There have been difficult patches, many of them due to the passing of family and friends, and we've had our differences of opinion. But from my vantage point, I couldn't have been luckier than to find her.

In the end, the only things that count are having a loving partner and enjoying wonderful children and grandchildren.

Dear Ian

> *Dear First Born,*
> *I've always loved you best because you were our first miracle. You were the genesis of a marriage and the fulfillment of young love. You sustained us through the hamburger years, the first apartment, our first mode of transportation (1955 Feet), and the seven-inch* TV *we paid on for 36 months. You were new, had unused grandparents, and enough clothes for a set of triplets. You were the original model for a mom and dad who were trying to work the bugs out. You got the strained lamb, the open safety pins and three-hour naps. You were the beginning!*
> —Erma Bombeck, from "*I've Always Loved You Best*"

On March 6, 1962, Evelyn and I began our life as parents when Ian Jeffrey Gold arrived.

Our lives would never be the same.

I suppose all young parents find it hard to believe that they can really raise a child. I remember watching Ian, those first few nights back from the hospital, to make sure he was breathing. One often hears parents say, "When you were sick, I didn't sleep a wink!" With Ian, I experienced the grain of truth in that old cliché.

In late 1967, during our year in New York, five-year-old Ian developed both chicken pox and scarlet fever at the same time. He probably picked them up in the Raggedy Andy kindergarten in our apartment building in Queens.

Joel, Josie, and Ian on the occasion of Ian's bar mitzvah, 1976.

Ian's graduation from McGill, Place des Arts. From left: Joel, Ev, Josie, Bubbie Chana, Ian, me, Zaidie Jack, Bubbie Rose.

His fever soared, and one of the pox on his upper chest became infected. A local pediatrician, hearing the desperation in my voice, made a house call—and wouldn't accept payment for his services. Despite my qualms about the American medical system, my own experience tells me there are decent doctors, indeed decent people, everywhere.

Ian went on a course of penicillin and, once again, I sat beside his bed all night. By morning his fever broke and both Ev and I could breathe again. A scar from that infected pox is still visible today.

Every weekend while we lived in New York, the four of us visited as many of the great sites of the city as we could. We wandered through museums, galleries, parks, Times Square, Rockefeller Center, went up the Empire State Building, took the ferries to Liberty and Ellis Islands, and we visited pretty much every historical site we could think of. The kids soaked it all in. One week I told Ian and Josie that we were about to cross the famous Verrazano-Narrows Bridge to Staten Island. Ian got really excited about that—then fell asleep in the car before we got there.

Back in Montreal, Ian was the first of our clan to attend Solomon Schechter Academy (SSA, formerly Shaare Zion Academy). Ev and I had different opinions about Jewish day schools, but happily her opinion prevailed. Solomon Schechter was a great place for our children. And their cousins were there: Clara and Murray's two older children, Elaine and Howard, were students there already, and their third, Steven, started grade one with Ian.

The philosopher at work, mid-1990s.

From very early on, it was clear that Ian was a bright and inquisitive child, as his sister and brother would be. But his table manners—more like under-the-table manners—could be a problem in restaurants. As a result, I learned the art of making up stories on the spot that would capture his attention. And, indeed, years later with our grandchildren, this became our version of The Neverending Story.

As I've written, Ian, Josie, and Joel all learned how to ride bicycles, and also to ski and skate. The boys played hockey, and if Josie had wanted to, I suspect she would have been a pretty good player too. Evelyn and I spent a lot of time standing in rinks and at the bottom of ski hills freezing our butts off while applauding our offspring! But we loved it. The skill of our children was thrilling for us.

Ian was a terrific older brother to Josie and Joel. Once, when he was eight, he went to pick up five-year-old Josie at a friend's house. Her mother called that evening to relate how Ian had reminded Josie to say "Thank you" as they left.

Ian was a keen observer, negotiator, and philosopher from a very early age. One evening my mother-in-law, Chana, was looking after the kids. Ian wasn't behaving well. When she said his parents would hear about it, Ian offered his grandmother a deal. "If you don't tell about me, I won't tell about you." I think it worked.

Ian was also a straight talker. When my Ph.D. diploma arrived in the mail a few weeks after convocation, Ian's incredulous comment was, "All that shushing for just one piece of paper?"

Not long after Joel was born in 1969, the boys shared a bedroom for many years, and Ian would make sure both beds were made before leaving for school. I watched Ian grow from strength to strength through Solomon Schechter, Herzliah High School, Marianopolis CEGEP, and later on at McGill and Princeton.

Ian chose to major in philosophy. But Ev and I were taken aback one Friday night, partway through Ian's undergraduate degree, when he announced that he was taking a year off to work in a parking lot. That didn't seem like a great idea to me. "Dropping out is easy," I told him, but "dropping back in is much harder." Happily he agreed, remained in school, and completed his degree in honours philosophy. His convocation ceremony was memorable: he graduated with the Prince of Wales medal in philosophy and went up to receive his medal and degree wearing what might be termed "leisure dress." For his Ph.D. graduation ceremony at Princeton, he managed to locate a jacket and tie.

At Princeton, Ian met Natalie, a fellow graduate student in philosophy from Australia. They got married in Sydney in 1998 and began working in Canberra, where Natalie was born. Alex (Django) and Adam arrived in 1998 and 2003, respectively. Evelyn and I logged a great many air miles during those years!

After about a decade Down Under, Ian called one evening to tell us he'd be in Montreal to give "some talks at McGill."

"Terrific!" I said. "Your room is available."

A few weeks after his visit, I ran into a colleague, Rebecca Feurer, the chair of epidemiology at McGill.

"So is he coming or not?" she asked.

"Is who coming where?" I replied.

Ian, it turned out, had been offered the Canada Research Chair in philosophy and psychiatry at McGill. Rebecca was chairing the search committee.

My immediate response was confusion: why hadn't he told us?

Ian explained, quite reasonably, that he didn't want to get our hopes up until the offer to Natalie had been clarified and confirmed.

Happily, Ian and Natalie were both hired as associate professors of philosophy, and not too long after their move to McGill, Natalie was named chair of the Department of Philosophy, a post now held by Ian.

As Django observed: "Daddy works for Mommy day and night."

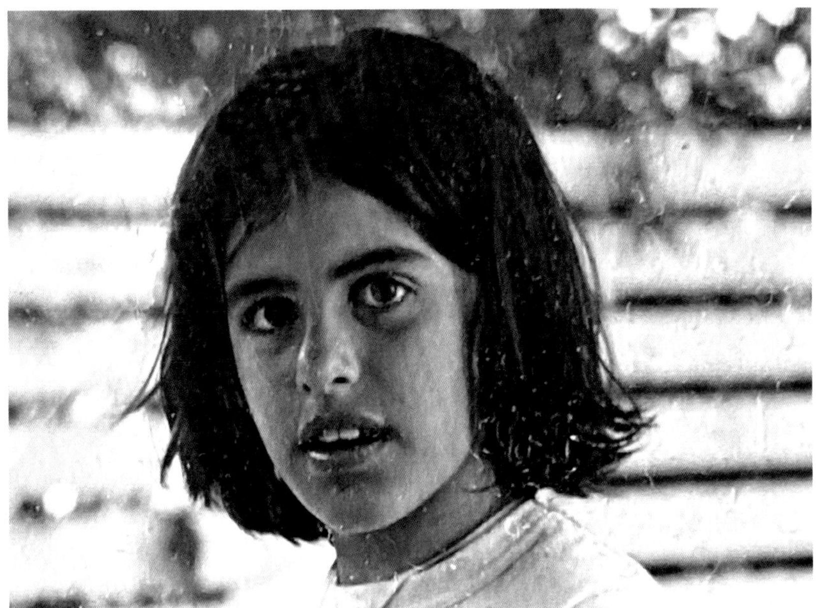

Josie, age eight.

Dear Josie

> *Dear Middle Born,*
> *I've always loved you the best because you drew a tough spot in the family and it made you stronger for it. You cried less, had more patience, wore faded hand-me-downs, and never in your life did anything first. But it only made you more special. You were the one we relaxed with, who helped us realize a dog could kiss you and you wouldn't get sick. You could cross a street by yourself long before you were old enough to get married. And you helped us understand the world wouldn't collapse if you went to bed with dirty feet. You were the child of our busy, ambitious years. Without you, we never could have survived the job changes and the tedium and routineness that is marriage.*
> —Erma Bombeck, from "*I've Always Loved You Best*"

Josie's arrival on February 24, 1965, heralded a new era in parenting for Ev and me. To state the obvious: boys and girls are different!

Josie was a contented child. She could spend a good part of the day playing happily by herself. She showed artistic talent as soon as she could hold a coloured pencil and her interest in the arts blossomed as she grew. She had the kind of confidence that can't be taught. From a very young age, she did the things she wanted to do, and with aplomb.

Josie's graduation from York, late 1980s. This was the first time I met Cleve, and it was about 150 degrees that day. I believe Josie's main thought was, *Get me the f—- out of here!*

When Josie was a toddler in New York, she came down with chicken pox—no doubt a gift from her brother Ian. When she was healing, I had a meeting in Atlantic City, and we took Josie for a stroll on the boardwalk. There we ran into a colleague, Dr. Rosalyn Yalow, who was there for the same conference. At the time, she was working on the radioimmunoassay technique for insulin, for which she would win a Nobel Prize. Josie and Rosalyn had a lovely conversation.

Back in Montreal, it was then six-year-old Josie's turn to learn how to ride a bike in the churchyard across from our home on Parkhaven Avenue.

Before I could take hold of the seat to keep her balanced, she had jumped on and pedalled away without the slightest hesitation. A few laps of the churchyard were all she needed to become an expert rider—at which point she peeled back in my direction, came to a perfect stop, and offered to teach *me*! A few wobbly, false starts later, Josie shouting encouragement the whole time, I managed to ride around the courtyard twice. I missed my bicycling window as a boy—but I was overjoyed to find this new one with my little girl.

Another time, Josie came home crying from the park around the corner from our house, saying one of the boys had "broken my doll's carriage." I quickly inspected the intact carriage, then took her back to the park to tell the young man to behave better. I found the perpetrator sitting in the dirt, holding his stomach and crying.

"It was him," she said, pointing.

I helped the boy up—he was about the same age as Josie—dusted him off, and asked what happened.

"I touched her doll carriage and she punched me!" he said, wiping off his tears.

New York, early 1990s. At the time, Ian was at Princeton, Joel was at Brown, and Josie and Cleve were in Toronto. Every year, to help them stay in touch and give them a short break from their studies, Ev and I would give them a weekend getaway in New York. They would go to amazing restaurants, attend plays, and go to museums (my children aren't big shoppers). They loved these weekends so much (Josie calls them a highlight of her life) they kept doing them whenever they could.

I went back home soon after. Josie could look after herself!

When Josie turned twelve, she and Ev began to have occasional differences of opinion about all the usual teenage issues. Driving home from work during those years, I often wondered what the issue of the day would be.

"What happened?" I'd say to Ev, shrugging my shoulders after hearing details of the latest fracas. "She was so easy as a child." Ev would nod and look at the ceiling. "She's definitely not a child anymore."

Then one day when she was about fifteen, Josie came to breakfast with a big smile.

"Good morning, everyone," she said.

Everyone looked up, surprised. I was stunned.

"Where have you been for the past three years?" I asked.

Josie just smiled.

A few years later we decided to sell our house and move closer to the hospital and McGill. Ian had already moved out, and Josie was about to move to Toronto to study fine arts at York University, and would go on to become a superb graphic designer. But the idea of her parents moving really bothered her.

"Our house is a meeting place for all my friends," she protested. "Now I'll never see anyone again."

Joel was avidly of the same opinion.

When prospective buyers came to inspect our home, Josie refused to leave her room.

"Their problem," she would say.

Josie and Joel needn't have worried. Many of Josie's friends were now studying nearby at McGill, so our new home stayed at the centre of things. And Joel's younger friends found the convenience of a "downtown meeting place" much to their liking.

Ian, who had already moved into an apartment on Saint Urbain Street, would listen to these arguments, shrug, and never take sides!

Over the next four years I was often in Toronto at the National Cancer Institute of Canada (NCIC), which made visiting Josie fun and easy.

On one trip, she invited me to dinner.

"Dad," she said, "I've made two things: fish and reservations."

On another occasion, we met for dinner at a downtown "businessman's hotel" where I and other NCIC committee members often lodged. I left my room key at the front desk so she could change, if she wanted to, before going down to dinner. In the restaurant we ordered some wine, talked about family matters and her classes, and enjoyed our food. But after a while I started noticing some of the older men at other tables glancing our way with subtly scornful expressions. What did they think was going on here?

It was an awkward moment for me, but I thought, *Well, if my daughter doesn't notice, I won't mention it.* But clearly she had. The bill came and I paid it.

"Shall we go back to the room, dear?" she said archly, and loud enough for everyone in the restaurant to hear. I cracked up.

As the folks around us realized we were father and daughter, they began to laugh too.

You're a lucky man, one couple said. No arguing with that!

Another great Josie story, for me, involves budgeting. Before Josie moved to Toronto, Ev explained the importance of monthly budgeting to her and the manner in which it should be done.

The next time Evelyn and I were in Toronto, she and Josie went shopping in Yorkville, an upscale and expensive shopping area, and we agreed to meet for lunch. As I walked down the street to meet them, they came toward me carrying a multitude of bags. Shopping had, clearly, been good. Josie lifted one bag at a time and showed me her budget: "This would be my budget for January, this for February, and on and on. Budgeting lesson learned!"

While in school at York, Josie met a young man by the name of Cleve Ziegler, who was at the University of Toronto, completing medical school. Evelyn and I had heard about Cleve from Josie, but we first met him at Josie's graduation ceremony. I was given strict instructions: the only topics I was allowed to discuss were baseball and the weather.

I shook the young man's hand.

"Beautiful weather for baseball," I said, blowing it in one sentence.

Cleve was lovable from the get-go and has remained that way. Josie and Cleve were married at the Shaare Zion Synagogue in Montreal in 1991. Cleve became the "politically conservative" branch of our family and has a terrific sense of humour, including a knack for languages and accents. He keeps us all laughing at Shabbat dinners. But he's no kidder in the operating room: Cleve is a master of gynecological surgery. Like all of our children, he has a gift for his profession.

One of the unexpected treasures of Josie moving to Toronto, for me, was getting to know my sister, Malk, better than ever. Malk and her husband, David Markus, were living in Toronto with their four sons during those years. I got to know my sister through the eyes of my daughter—and they were so much alike. David informs me that on Friday evenings, he'd regularly come home to find Malk and Josie already through their first bottle of good red wine. Malk still insists to "her brother the doctor" that wine is the only thing that *really* relieves pain.

Malk and Josie are more than aunt and niece: they're good friends, and they've remained close in the years since the Markus family moved to Los Angeles. When Josie called her aunt to tell her that she was pregnant with her fourth child, Matthew, the response was pure Malk:

"Are you out of your fucking mind?"

Dear Joel

> *To My Baby,*
> *I've always loved you best because while endings are generally sad, you are such a joy!! You readily accepted the mild-stained bibs, the lower bunk, the cracked baseball bat, the baby book that had nothing written in it except a recipe for graham-cracker piecrust that someone had jammed between the pages. You are the one we held on to so tightly. You darkened our hair, quickened our steps, squared our shoulders, restored our vision, and gave us a sense of humor that security, maturity, and durability can't provide. When your hairline takes on the shape of Lake Erie and your own children tower over you, you will still be our baby!!!*
> —Erma Bombeck, from *"I've Always Loved You Best"*

By the time Joel came along on January 3, 1969, Evelyn and I were comfortable in our roles as parents. I didn't worry about his breathing through the night, as I had with Ian, and even in Joel's preteens I let him cross the road alone. Joel was conceived during our sojourn in New York, the city where he has now lived and worked for decades, and as I mentioned, he still occasionally jokes that we should have stayed south of the border until he was born so he wouldn't have had to wait years to obtain his green card and American citizenship.

Joel and the usual suspects at my and Evelyn's 25th wedding anniversary, 1985. Joel says he was drunk. No matter. It was a party!

As a toddler, Joel really enjoyed standing up in restaurant booths and throwing dinner rolls at unsuspecting diners on the other side. It made us very popular.

Joel was obviously competitive as a child. He had to be the best at what he did, whether in the classroom or on the hockey rink, and that has continued into his adult life.

He attended Solomon Schechter Academy and Herzliah High School, like his brother and sister. Joel was a *great* student, made a lot of friends, and spoke his mind. And he became the most avid hockey player of the group, although Josie matched him as a fan in cheering on the Canadiens. Larry Charney, a good friend and one of Joel's coaches, remembers him well: "Joel was one of the kids who actually did what you asked him to do." Joel continued to play hockey for years with the "old guys."

When it came time for university, it was clear Joel would do his undergraduate degree out of town. He was accepted by Ivy League schools Yale, Harvard, Brown, and Princeton, so the only question was picking "the one." Joel liked Princeton, but with Ian already there pursuing his Ph.D., Joel felt his parents would probably be calling a little too often to make sure he and his brother were eating Friday dinner together. And Yale was not Joel's favourite. That left Harvard and Brown.

LEFT: Joel's graduation photo from Brown.

RIGHT: Joel at home.

To help him decide, Joel visited the two campuses. I imagined Harvard would prove attractive, but Joel returned home set on Brown. His reason? When he arrived at Brown, someone helped him carry his bag!

Brown worked out extremely well. Unlike other institutions where teaching assistants do much of the teaching, Brown maintained the tradition of professors giving lectures, resulting in a highly engaged student body and good connections between students and professors.

In 1990, after taking a course in neuroscience at Brown, Joel spent a semester abroad at University College London (UCL) doing research on the anatomy of the visual cortex in a superb lab headed by Semir Zeki.

"Dad," he said over the phone from England, "I'm getting negative data, what do I do?"

"You publish it!" I said. "Negative data is just as good as positive results. You have to share what's been explored and shown to be unproductive so that other directions can be taken. Otherwise you can chase and chase and chase for years. Negative data is essential."

When we visited Joel in London, I felt sure neuroscience would prove to be his métier. But after graduating from Brown, Joel proved interested in medical school, and to our delight he applied to and was accepted by McGill. He and some friends rented an apartment in Mile End, about six blocks north of my old haunts. Invited for breakfast one Sunday, we learned the rule of the house: no dish would be washed until all had been used!

Because Joel was entering a medical program in which I played a part, it was important that we not interact in any significant fashion. Joel needed space to forge his own way into medicine and everyone agreed the best approach was, quite simply, no contact. Joel was never to be assigned to a hospital or specialty where he and I might meet in any professional capacity. This turned out to be a great guideline, simple and easy to enforce.

One summer evening when Evelyn and I were at the cottage in Trout Lake, the phone rang. It was Joel. His tone was sombre.

"You're going to be unhappy," he said.

"Oh goodness," I said, bracing for the worst. I motioned to Evelyn to come to the phone.

"Okay, tell us what happened."

"I've decided to become a psychiatrist."

"Oh. Is that all?"

"Well, I know you think psychiatry is kind of a nerdy field…"

"Don't be silly, that's great! Whatever you choose is fine with us."

Another time, I received a call from a physician at the Jewish General Hospital who had Joel on his service. Many of Joel's teachers have been very complimentary over the years so I was half-expecting him to say that Joel was a bright guy, or something along those lines. But I was wrong. He'd called me to say that my son was "a very decent person" and that we should be proud of him.

And I was. Smarts are great—but decency is much more important. Once you've studied long enough it's not that difficult to be a good doctor, but it's a lot harder to be a *kind* doctor. Kindness is easily lost in the midst of an intense day.

After finishing medical school at McGill, Joel made his way to Bellevue Hospital in New York for his training in psychiatry, remaining there for several years before transferring his teaching to Mount Sinai Hospital in New York City. By then, he had also moved into his own office and private practice. Evelyn and I are delighted by how much Joel enjoys the practice he has.

Along the way, Joel met Cathy Vignola in Montreal, who joined him in New York, and they got married a few years later. For reasons of which only they are aware, the marriage didn't work out well. But the important factor was the adoption of Amalia, who made it all seem worthwhile.

Ian and Joel share a great many interests. Indeed, they have even published an important book together, entitled *Suspicious Minds: How Culture Shapes Madness*. On the Internet, their shared Twitter handle is @ThinkVsShrink.

Taken together, Evelyn and I have been extraordinarily fortunate to have wonderful, talented, and loving children who have remained devoted to us and to each other.

My incredible family, gathered for my eightieth birthday celebration at Chateau Montebello, 2016. Front left: Michael, Zack, Matthew, Joel, Amalia. Middle: Josie, Ev, Benji, Adam, Natalie. Back: Cleve, me, Alex, Ian.

Dear Grandchildren

As I write this memoir, there are seven of you.

In the Gold–Ziegler family there are Zack, Michael, Benji, and Matthew. In the Stoljar–Gold family, there are Alex (Django) and Adam. And finally there is Joel's daughter, our one granddaughter, Amalia.

This memoir, my dear grandchildren, is for you.

I've thought long and hard about writing about each of you. But that would require seven books!

So please know this: I love you beyond what simple words can describe.

You have brought me infinite joy, and I know that I speak for your Bubbie in this as well. We wouldn't change a single thing about any of you.

I've had the privilege of telling you our version of The Neverending Story. I trust that it will always end with "And they all lived happily ever after."

One of you once made the comment "You love Zack more." As I've told you, we've loved Zack longer because he arrived first. But there is no difference in our love to each of you. Your hugs are beyond value. We look forward to each squeeze.

We know that each of you will go on to do great things. Zack and Michael in law, Benji in finance, and Alex in medicine. Adam and Matthew and Amalia have yet to decide, but we know you will choose well. On Trout Lake, in younger days, each of you chose your own special stone. We put them in the tumbler, cleaned and polished them together, and they became your own. In a sense, you are like those agates. You are unique.

Thank you, each of you, for being *you*.

Journal: Friday Evening Dinner

Sunday, January 22, 2017

Dinner this past Friday was like most Friday-evening dinners in recent memory. With Joel and Amalia in New York, there were twelve at the table: Bubbie and me, the six Gold–Zeiglers (Josie, Cleve, Zack, Michael, Benji, and Matt) and the four Stoljar–Golds (Ian, Natalie, Alex, and Adam). In the kitchen, there were the usual hors d'oeuvres ("Never eat on an empty stomach," as the saying goes) before everyone arrived. Then I watched Bubbie, with Adam and Matt, light the Sabbath candles and say the blessing, and then we all headed to the dining room. Cleve blessed the wine, with many at the table chipping in, then Matt and Addie said the blessing over the challah and passed it and other dishes around as conversation started.

With so many at one table, there are always multiple conversations. To avoid disputes, I asked for a ban on political conversations, which have become more heated in the age of Trump. From the head of the table, I could hear snippets of them all: tennis at the Australian Open, movies old and new, varying opinions about the boys' teachers. Adam has recently had his bar mitzvah—a great success. Natalie's family was here from Australia, enjoyed their stay, and are all now safely home. All the boys had good fall semesters, and Zack received early acceptance to law school at Queen's University (though I feel certain he'll go to McGill, which is his preference).

All of this was wonderful. The people seated around the table that evening, along with Joel and Amalia in New York, are those I love most in the world. But they are also the ones who keep me up a good deal at night. Have I done enough for them, as a father, as a grandfather?

And so I considered each of the members of my immediate family again, in turn: my wife, my children, my son-in-law, daughter-in-law, and all my grandchildren. Each has very special qualities, and abilities beyond any I've ever had. They will do things I can't even imagine. I'm sorry that I likely won't be around to see as many of their successes as I might wish. But with all that said, I still feel very proud.

Evelyn Gold, *Sir Isaak Walton Killam Boulevard*. In the mid-1980s when we told Bubbie Chana that we were moving to the Boulevard (pictured above), she kept asking "what boulevard, what boulevard?" She was a little deaf by then. Ev decided to name her painting after the Killam Prize, which I received in 1985. "It paid for our house, didn't it?" My wife has a sense of humour.

TOP LEFT: At the Wailing Wall, Jerusalem.

TOP RIGHT: Ian and Natalie.

BOTTOM: Me and Ev looking trim.

Canadian Medical Hall of Fame induction, 2010.

Phil Gold, 1978. This photo was taken when Sam Freedman and I won the Gairdner International Award for our discovery of carcinoembryonic antigen and for studies "which elucidated its biological and clinical significance."

PART V

A Career in Medicine

The McGill Cancer Centre

Sometime in 1975 I received a call from Sam Freedman, then dean of medicine at McGill.

"Phil, could you use more lab space?" he asked.

"Do I need to breathe?" I replied, laughing. It was a shared joke: we both knew my lab on the tenth floor of the Montreal General had been overcrowded for several years by then.

A few days later on Pine Avenue, I met several colleagues from the lab, including Joe Shuster and John Krupey, to inspect our prospective new digs: the entire seventh floor of the McIntyre Medical Sciences Building.

Over the previous decade, the space had been home to many projects, including research into cancer cell metabolism. Sam understood our work was growing in importance, and he wanted to help us succeed. Over the next months, Evelyn and the McGill construction group renovated the entire floor, and in 1976 the McGill Cancer Centre (MCC) was opened with me as its inaugural director.

The creation of the MCC allowed us to recruit brilliant young researchers. Abraham (Abe) Fuks, who'd trained in medicine and immunology at McGill and was doing postdoctoral studies at Harvard, returned to the MCC. Cliff Stanners was recruited from the University of Toronto. Cliff's student Nicole Beauchemin joined him: she was in the process of finishing her Ph.D. and would have a brilliant career at the MCC. These three, along with Joe Shuster, John Krupey, and Chaim Banjo, performed groundbreaking work in defining the CEA family of genes in the 1990s.

Another key purpose in establishing the MCC was to position McGill internationally as a leading cancer research centre. And it worked: after a decade of development, McGill, and Montreal universities in general, achieved a critical mass of cancer investigators who could interact easily with each

The Rosalind and Morris Goodman Cancer Institute in 2021. The path on the right connects this new building to the seventh floor of the McIntyre Medical Sciences Building, where the McGill Cancer Centre got its start in 1976 with me as inaugural director.

other, and with colleagues internationally, to refine and expand their ideas. The results speak for themselves: the MCC has produced superb, award-winning cancer research and remarkable people. Among its early researchers, Abe Fuks became dean of medicine in 1995 and Cliff Stanners took on the directorship of the MCC in 1988 before retiring to become a vintner in southern Ontario. Nicole Beauchemin continues to do great work at the centre.

After twenty-five years in the McIntyre Building, the McGill Cancer Centre expanded again—this time into an adjacent new structure built expressly for the MCC. This was made possible by an endowment from the Rosalind and Morris Goodman family in 2008. Years earlier, I had doodled designs on napkins for such a building, and it finally happened under the directorship of Michel Tremblay. The McGill Cancer Centre was renamed the Rosalind and Morris Goodman Cancer Centre, which in 2021 became the Rosalind and Morris Goodman Cancer *Institute*. Under the direction of Dr. Morag Park, renowned investigators such as Nahum Sonenberg continue to lead the way in global cancer research from the Goodman Institute.

Adventures with Sheila Kussner

One morning in 1979, at the McGill Cancer Centre (MCC), a very interesting woman walked into my office unannounced.

"Take this or my husband will kill me," she said, handing me an unmarked envelope.

Slightly alarmed, I took it. Inside was a very substantial cheque, in the thousands, made out to the centre.

"Please sit down," I said, offering her a chair. "Madam, if I may ask, what is your name?"

"Sheila Kussner."

I knew her name: Sheila's philanthropic work in the community was already something of a legend, and in the coming years she would found Hope and Cope at the Jewish General Hospital, a pioneering cancer support organization for patients and families. But we had never met.

"This is an incredibly generous gift," I said. "To what do we owe this donation?"

Sheila liked to play the stock market, she said, but her husband, Marvin, didn't approve of the habit—so she had to get rid of the money. She'd heard the new cancer centre was showing great promise and wanted to support it. I thanked her profusely, and we talked for a while about my ambitions for the MCC.

"I love the sound of all that," she said. "But, Phil, you know you're going to need a lot of money to achieve those goals. And not just grant money."

"I know you raise funds for the Jewish General," I said. "But would you consider doing the same for us at McGill?"

Sheila liked the idea, so we walked downstairs to the office of Richard Cruess, dean of medicine, and apprised him of the plan. Dick also liked the idea. We said our goodbyes and left it to Sheila to put things in motion.

The matter might have ended there, but a few days later Sheila called.

"What do you have at the dean's office in the afternoon?"

"You mean what meetings?"

"No, to eat and drink."

"Whatever's left in the coffee pot?" I replied.

"Oh no, that won't do," she said. "We'll have it catered."

"Have what catered?"

"Phil, is wine allowed at a university meeting?"

"I really don't know. Let me ask the dean."

Dean Cruess okayed the wine.

A few weeks later, a local caterer arrived on the seventh floor of the McIntyre Building, accompanied by a blue-and-gold waistcoated waiter. They laid out a tablecloth on what was normally a generic meeting-room table and busily began setting placemats and laying out food. Dick walked in, looking a bit surprised.

"Don't worry," I said. "Sheila knows what she's doing. I'm sure."

Soon, eight more guests arrived, each representing considerable philanthropy. And then Sheila appeared bearing homemade *schnecken*, her favourite dessert.

"Dean, would you mind pouring the wine?"

Ready for anything, Dick got up and poured the wine.

The meeting progressed. Perhaps twenty minutes later, Sheila repeated her request.

"Dean, would you mind pouring the wine?"

Dick was about to get up again when I put my hand on his arm.

"Don't," I whispered. "The waiter's name is Dean. It's embroidered on his waistcoat."

My adventures with Sheila continued for decades to come. All told, she raised some $35 million for the McGill Department of Oncology and its research arm at the cancer centre (now Goodman Cancer Institute). It's no exaggeration to say these owe their existence and ever-increasing success to her. In recognition of her outstanding contributions, McGill awarded Sheila Kussner with an honorary degree. At the convocation, and to great amusement, Dick Cruess told the story of the wine-serving confusion.

Physician-in-Chief

In 1979, after more than twenty years at the reins of the Department of Medicine, Doug Cameron stepped down as physician-in-chief of the Montreal General Hospital. His tenure had been a time of great change in the organization of departments of medicine, and the teaching of medicine internationally. For his contributions to the faculty, McGill established the Douglas G. Cameron Chair in Medicine.

In the subsequent weeks, as the question of Doug's replacement came up, I was invited to meet with the search committee seeking his replacement. A number of physicians had already been interviewed and the committee wanted my thoughts on the kind of person they should be recruiting. After a rather long discussion, I was truly surprised, a few days later, when I was offered the post. When I hesitated, the chair of the committee suggested I take the weekend to decide.

The McGill Cancer Centre had been established only four years earlier and things were really beginning to roll there. I was loath to give that up. But while discussing the matter with Evelyn, a range of other considerations came up. Most particularly, the possibility of playing a significant role in updating some of the hospital's norms in light of the times. Historically, the Montreal General had not been particularly welcoming to Jewish staff.

It was certainly *not* as horrific as 1934's "Days of Shame" that began across town at Notre Dame Hospital. This was the infamous incident when the

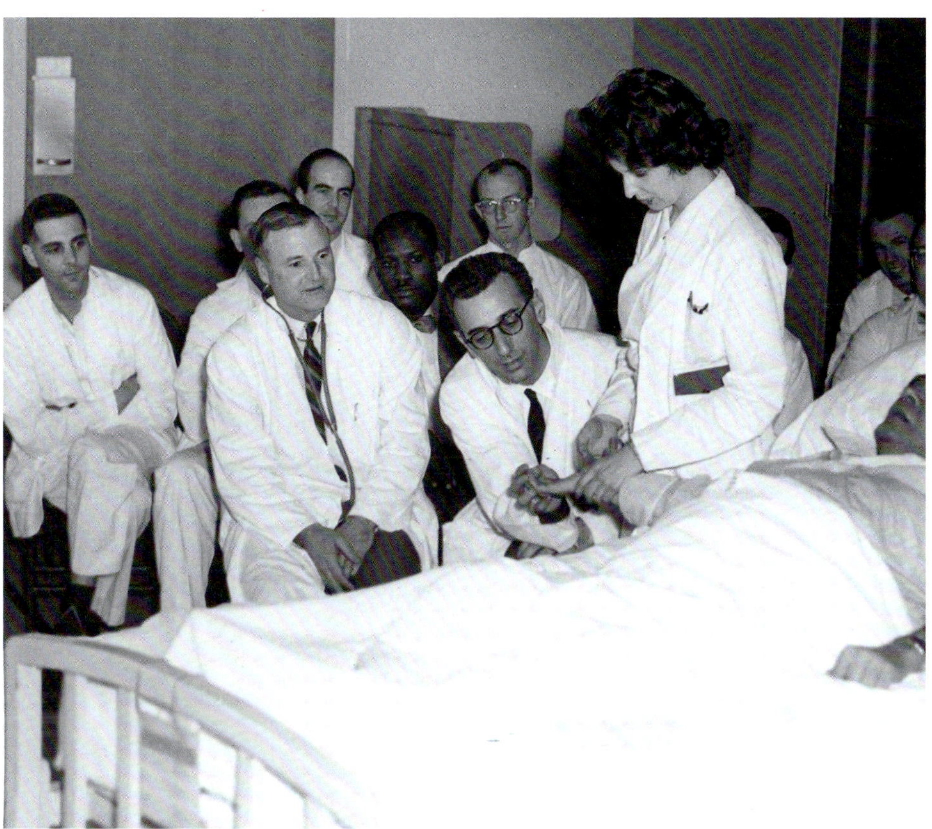

Douglas Cameron (seated, front left) in 1967, leading resident rounds with my former mentor Arnold Burgen (foreground, with glasses). The standing woman, a rare female resident at the time, is presenting the case to Arnold, who is double-checking the patient's fingers for paleness, a telltale sign of anemia. Doug Cameron had the bright idea of creating specialty divisions within the Department of Medicine, with research labs, patient wards, and physicians teaching clinics all grouped together. When I succeeded him as physician-in-chief, I made that idea a reality.

hiring of Dr. Sam Rabinovitch, a top medical-school graduate from the Université de Montréal, resulted in the resignation of the entire resident staff at Notre Dame and all francophone hospitals in Montreal—because a Jew had been hired instead of a French-Canadian. Rabinovitch resigned to put an end to the developing crisis in patient care. He relocated to St. Louis, Missouri, to obtain his training in internal medicine before returning to Montreal. Interestingly, Evelyn had worked in Sam Rabinovitch's medical laboratory as a technician before we were married.

But back to the Montreal General. After having spent twenty years in the classrooms, the laboratories, the clinics, and the wards of the General, I knew first-hand how things had changed. Indeed, Doug Cameron had recruited a number of excellent new staff without consideration for their religion or ethnicity. These included Arnold Burgen as deputy director of the University Medical Clinic; Charles Hollenberg, who would go on to be provost at the University of Toronto; my early supporter Sam Freedman, who was now dean of medicine at McGill; and Harvey Barkun, the hospital's CEO, with whom I'd had many discussions in Yiddish. ("You know, Harvey, if things

From humble beginnings come great things.

LEFT: the Montreal General Hospital in 1823, with a wrought-iron fence donated by John Molson, Sr., in its original building at the corner of Craig Street (today Rue St-Antoine) and St. Lawrence Boulevard.

RIGHT: the MGH in 2020 on the slopes of Mount Royal. The General was the first teaching hospital in Canada, and is part of the reason McGill exists today.

go wrong in medicine at McGill, we're looking at a pogrom," I sometimes joked with him in our *mameloshn* or mother-tongue.)

So perhaps I could contribute positively to the Department of Medicine and the hospital as a whole. However, the most important issue was my suitability for the position. I'd never really been an administrator, nor did I want to be one, despite my activities at the cancer centre. Daily paperwork would be an essential part of the role. Was I the right person for the job? Evelyn made the crucial observations: "You took on the cancer centre and made it work. You also have clear views about the hospital's needs. And you know the players."

That settled it!

I accepted the post and in 1980 became the first Jewish physician-in-chief of the Montreal General Hospital and, indeed, the first Douglas G. Cameron Professor of Medicine at McGill. And so began the next fifteen years of my career.

I moved from my seventh-floor office in the Immunology/Allergy division to Doug's old office on the sixth floor. This was a spacious complex of rooms that included a front office for a secretary, a library–conference room that doubled as Evelyn's office (when she volunteered her time), my office next to that, and an unused side room with a sink that needed changing.

To celebrate my new job, that summer my daughter, Josie, gave me a lovely olivewood mezuzah that she had purchased in Israel on a school trip. Because the doorframe of my new office was metal, I called the Carpentry Department for help. The hospital carpenter Waldo, an old acquaintance, arrived soon after to install it.

"The screws I'm going to use are brass, a mixed metal," he said. "Is it okay to use them on a Jewish religious article?"

It was a rather surprising variation on *shatnez*, the admonition in Jewish religious law not to dress in mixed fibres: "You shall not wear combined fibres, wool and linen together." Although not a problem, to show my ap-

Oswald Wellisch, chief carpenter at the Montreal General. Whenever I had a problem I called Oswald. "Go for lunch," he'd say, "it'll be done when you come back."

preciation for Waldo's concern I called an old friend and my go-to person in all things rabbinical, the late Michael Herschorn. At the time, Michael was chair of the Department of Mathematics and dean of students at McGill.

"Where is this mezuzah going to be put?" he asked.

"On the door frame of my office at the Montreal General," I told him.

"At the Montreal General? Even with crazy glue," he said.

Even my brilliant, dear old friend considered a mezuzah at the General extraordinary.

In my new office, I also inherited Doug Cameron's secretary, Yvonne Wall, a very pleasant woman who apparently had the habit of stacking any paperwork she hadn't completed that day in an ever-growing pile beside her desk. But one day after Ev heard her being very rude to a patient on the telephone, I had a chat with Dean Cruess and told him that one of us had to be gone the next day. Dick found a new placement for Yvonne at the McIntyre Building.

Her replacement, the efficient and pleasant Liane Arbour, was joined by the delightful Anna Cuccovia, who took over the side room when it became clear that it was a two-person job. Sometimes Anna had difficulty transcribing my dictation, to comic effect. Between the four of us in the suite, these became known as Anna-isms. One day, to my surprise, I heard Anna speaking on the phone loudly in Italian. When she was done, I asked what that was about. She told me she was speaking to the person in Italy who had arranged a symposium from which I had just returned. She told them, she explained, that she was ashamed I hadn't been reimbursed yet for my travel by a fellow Italian. A cheque was forthcoming the next week.

As I settled into my new job, it became clear that the Department of Medicine, by far the largest department in the hospital, could not be run by one person. I turned to three experienced colleagues who I knew could get the various jobs done.

Joe Shuster took over the Research Institute (formerly the University Medical Clinic). Joe, of course, was an old friend and colleague in the Division of Clinical Immunology and Allergy. He was an outstanding investigator, and someone with whom I shared all of my thoughts. Blair Whittemore took on the day-to-day operation of the medical wards. Blair was an excellent hematologist whom I'd known since our residency training. Totally committed to patient care, Blair was also a superbly organized person and a great teacher, and remains a good friend to this day. Peter McCloud, an excellent physician and teacher, agreed to manage the training of residents and students in our hospital training program. No troika has ever been better.

With key leadership in place, I turned to the hospital's budget. Hiring new full-time clinical teaching and research staff would require funding. I felt certain that Doug Cameron would have looked after these matters during his tenure. But like Old Mother Hubbard, when I looked in the cupboard, I found that the cupboard was bare. The staff that Doug had hired, for the most part, had their incomes from private practice outside the hospital. They had not been hired as clinician-teachers or clinician-scientists. Some form of permanent funding would have to be found to supplement the income of the full-time staff members I planned to recruit.

Dick Cruess said the Faculty of Medicine would help, and it did, in a big way. But for the hospital to remain truly viable as a teaching and research institute would require additional funds. I raised this issue at my first departmental staff meeting as physician-in-chief. I laid out the problem and explained that one of the few solutions I could see would be to start taxing all clinical earnings at 3 percent. Since all of the staff, regardless of their other academic activities, would have one or two clinics a week, the tax would be significant. There were some incredulous-looking faces around the room. "I realize how disturbing this may be," I said, "and I'm prepared to step down, if that's the wish of the staff. I'll step out for a few minutes to let you consider the matter." When I returned, the unanimous consensus was to accept my "three-percent solution." I assured the staff that the funds raised by taxing would be looked after by a committee of their choosing, to which I would submit the Department of Medicine's needs on an annual basis.

As I was told later, some members of the department were concerned that, with my background, I might expand research activities only. But since clinician-teachers were also involved, and the other plans looked promising, that was considered a step forward. The Clinical Teaching Units (CTUs) that Doug Cameron had proposed years earlier, but which he hadn't been able to establish, could now finally go forward.

Next on my list of major issues was the ongoing public–private split within the department. Despite the fact that Canada enjoyed universal health care, the hospital still had so-called "public" and "private" wards. The latter were wards where senior members of staff could admit their outside patients for such things as complete annual checkups. This effectively created a two-tiered system of care that was ripe for criticism and abuse. The practice had to be stopped and the situation reorganized.

Closely related to this issue was the problem of chaotic norms that had grown up around the teaching of our younger doctors or residents. Up to 1980, physicians in private practice outside the hospital would do a month or two of morning teaching on a medical ward, then go to their private clinics in the afternoon. This gave short shrift to pretty much all residents at the hospital, since there were no stable CTUs in place to deal with a host of specialties.

And so, with the funding more or less in hand, the restructuring began.

First, I had to thank the outside "private" physicians for their past service on the active teaching wards and replace them with physicians who would be at the hospital, full time, as clinician-teachers or clinician-scientists. I did this by inviting them to my office for coffee. After some chit-chat, I would thank them for their years of service to the hospital and to McGill. Then I explained the new rounding and teaching programs, and expressed the hope that they would be able to help their younger colleagues with this task. Liane Arbour, who took notes in these meetings and had a good sense of humour, often tried to guess how long it would take for someone to realize their teaching and rounding duties had just been terminated.

Then came the difficult task of reordering the physical space within the hospital, so that specialty divisions and their outpatient clinics could be housed as close together as possible. Given the rather random apportioning of space in the hospital over previous decades, this reorganization took several long years. For example, Cardiology and Gastroenterology needed space for specific types of frequent tests. More space was needed. With a somewhat heavy heart, I was able to relocate Family Medicine to St. Mary's Hospital and the Jewish General Hospital, where it would play a greater role. By the mid-1980s we had established true CTUs for more efficient care and better teaching. I was delighted by that accomplishment.

During the shuffle, I was also able to address the complete lack of a Division of General Internal Medicine at the hospital, that is, physicians able to address serious general medical problems with no clear need of a specific organ specialty, such as endocrinology or respirology. For years the absence

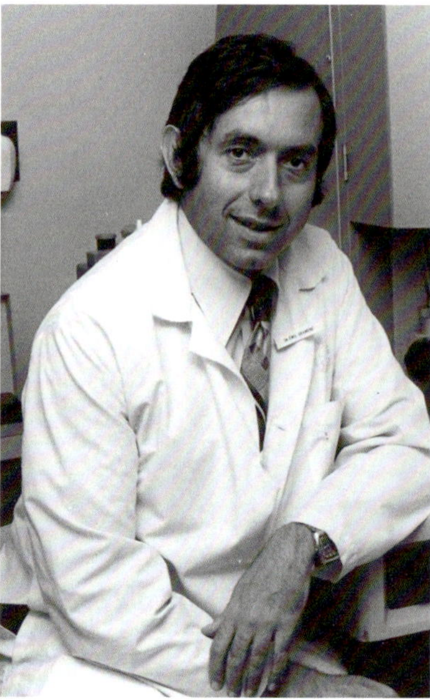

LEFT: Dr. Emil Skamene, MGH Research Institute, 1980. Emil founded the McGill Centre for the Study of Host Resistance in 1988, with a focus on immunogenetics. His work on mycobacteria (a major cause of tuberculosis and leprosy) won him and his team international acclaim.

RIGHT: Joseph Shuster, my brilliant colleague and long-time friend, led the Immunology and Allergy division for twenty-five years and also directed the Research Institute. We drove to work together for seventeen years. Joe had such a good effect on me that Evelyn often referred to him as my "sedative."

of such members of staff had bothered me. I was warned that Alec Miller, one of our best private physicians, would fight the idea of creating a division to do what he felt he already did pretty well on his own.

"He'll be fine with it," I told concerned staffers. "I've already asked him to be director of the division, and he has accepted."

A superb group of young internists (specialists in general internal medicine) was hired, with Alec's enthusiastic participation, and after a few years Alec was happy to pass on his directorship to Laurence Green, who had been my first chief resident and would later be my personal physician. Laurence is truly a doctor's doctor and a great teacher.

During my first five-year term as physician-in-chief, I tried to continue my work in the lab. But quite soon it became apparent there was no way to do both jobs well. And so, again with a heavy heart, I distributed the research grants I had had for many years. Happily the funds went to members of my research team, who have continued to obtain grant renewals successfully to the present day in their own labs under their own names.

I liked my position as physician-in-chief so well, and interacted well enough with my staff and our students, that I continued in the position for two more terms, for a total of fifteen years.

One final development is noteworthy. Some years earlier, the hospital had recruited Emil Skamene, a fine immunologist from Prague who, like me, wanted to establish a centre for innovative medicine. This would be a program wherein clinicians and scientists at the hospital and its research institute could carry out ethical clinical research that benefited from the modern facilities available at the McGill hospitals. This research would help physicians to develop and evaluate new treatments for some of the most critical diseases they were seeing. I put the idea of such a centre to Harvey Barkun, CEO of the hospital, and to the executive committees of the Staff Association, Research Institute, MGH Hospital Board, and the McGill faculty. All agreed it was a good idea and that a budget would be allocated if I could find the space for such an operation.

Here, I asked the help of Lorne Cassidy, an old friend whom I had brought on staff some years earlier. Lorne had worked as a physician in industry, and had a natural sense of organization. He had the delightful habit of standing in the sixth-floor atrium of the General and greeting staff in the morning. Indeed, the atrium was referred to as Cassidy's office, or "the Corridor of Power." Lorne and I found space at the end of the west wing on the thirteenth floor, restructured and renovated it, and the Centre for Innovative Medicine (CIM) was born.

After fifteen years as physician-in-chief at the Montreal General, with an overlapping five-year term as McGill chair of medicine, I left the post feeling that I had, indeed, made a contribution. I then made my way to the CIM, where I've spent a good part of the past twenty-five years. During this time Clinical Trials Research has taken on a new life at the hospital, and CIM activity has expanded both within the MGH and downtown at the Glen, the new home of the MUHC. I've also spent more time in the Division of Clinical Immunology and Allergy—seeing patients, training residents in the specialty, and teaching at undergrad and post-graduate levels.

When the pandemic began, my former student, then resident, now outstanding colleague in Clinical Immunology/Allergy, Dr. Geneviève Genest, urged me to leave the hospital. "Go home to Mrs. Gold with my love. I don't want to see you in the ICU." And so I did. But I remained active in the hospital division, by telephone and email, until June 2021, which took me to sixty years after my graduation from medical school. It seemed an appropriate time to retire with some degree of grace.

I continue to teach students at all levels, often via Zoom, which I'll do as long as health allows and any need for me exists. Of all the things I've done, other than parenting my children, teaching may leave the longest legacy. We reproduce ourselves biologically; but academically, we reproduce ourselves by teaching. I have *nachas* (pride and joy) from both!

In my new office on the thirteenth floor of the Montreal General, late 1990s, after the completion of my fifteen-year tenure as physician-in-chief. The MGH has been my workplace for over sixty years. I continue to teach today.

Administratum

I have no doubt that many people have had to deal with slow, bureaucratic administrations at one time or another. As physician-in-chief, changing outdated hospital norms was a daily frustration for me. To manage my own impatience, without causing offence, and to encourage change in a lighthearted manner, I began to toy with the idea of a chemical substance or element that caused this condition. Thus began my invention of the radioactive element Administratum, denoted by the letters Ad.

Now, as you're probably aware from lectures in basic chemistry, the atoms of all elements are composed of three major constituents: protons, neutrons, and electrons. And it's the electrons that initiate most chemical reactions.

Administratum, remarkably, has no electrons. It does, however, have a hundred protons and two hundred neutrons. In addition, each neutron has an associate neutron and at least two assistant neutrons, making it the heaviest element in the Periodic Table. In addition, Administratum has an associated and often interfering element, Secretarium, which requires tender loving care, such as the regular provision of coffee.

Since Administratum has no electrons, it cannot initiate any reaction on its own. But added to any other ongoing reaction, it either slows it down or stops it altogether.

Richard and Sylvia Cruess. After Richard served in the U.S. Navy Medical Corps, the couple moved to Montreal to pursue their respective specialties in orthopaedics and endocrinology. After fifteen years at the Royal Vic and the Shriners, Dick became dean of the Faculty of Medicine at McGill, 1981–1995. A Fellow of the Royal Society, Dick was made a Companion of the Order of Canada in 2014.

Whenever a particular project at the hospital slowed down, I would simply say, "So everyone has had an overdose of Administratum this week." That tended to get the action going again. No administrator enjoys being embarrassed.

Like all radioactive substances, Administratum decays with time. When it has lost all its activity, it transforms into a new element: Govenmentum, or Go.

A Word about Richard Cruess

I would be remiss in this memoir if I didn't say a word about Richard (Dick) Cruess.

Dick was born in London, Ontario, received his B.A. from Princeton, and met his wife, Sylvia, in medical school at Columbia. Sylvia would become a fine endocrinologist and later a hospital administrator. They chose McGill for their clinical training because they could be sure of having posts at the same hospital. After residency at the Royal Victoria Hospital and the New York Orthopedic Hospital, and three years with the Navy Medical Corps, Dick became an orthopedic surgeon at the Royal Victoria Hospital and later surgeon-in-chief at the Shriners Hospital in Montreal. From 1981 to 1995, Dick was an outstanding dean of medicine at McGill.

I first met Dick in 1980, when I was cleaning out my office at the cancer centre prior to taking on the post of physician-in-chief at the General.

"You're Phil Gold," he said as we passed in the hall outside his new office.

"Yes, I am," I replied, "and I have been for some time."

We laughed.

"Come on in," he said. "We should talk."

And talk we did, for two hours. He told me about his career path and family, I told him about mine. What was it like growing up Jewish in Montreal and at McGill? he asked, listening with interest and distress to the stories I told him. To his great credit, from then on, Dick took every opportunity to point out at faculty meetings not just how far McGill had come in overcoming antisemitism, but that we still had some way to go.

Throughout my years as physician-in-chief and chair of medicine, Dick had my back, and his support made my life so much easier than it might have been. We remain good friends to this day. A few times a year, when we meet for lunch, I always leave refreshed.

Awards of all kinds have been given to Dick Cruess for his medical excellence, but I would add one more: the Highest Award of Merit for *Menschlichkeit*. I have known few people more decent and deserving of such recognition.

*The Book of Jane**

I would also be remiss if I did not also say a word about a remarkable young woman named Jane Poulson, whom I got to know soon after I became physician-in-chief.

Jane Poulson was a singularity. Blind since her third year of medical school, as a complication of Type I juvenile diabetes, she not only completed her medical degree but told me that she wanted to continue her training. It was the only time I was glad that Jane couldn't see me, since I'm sure I blanched. But I promised her that I'd give it my best shot. With remarkable agreement from the necessary bodies at the Montreal General, provincially and nationally, and with the appropriate safeguards in place, Jane completed her years of training and breezed through her exams in internal medicine. One can only imagine the hardships she experienced, trying to keep up with her training while trying to adapt to her disability. But I never heard a word of complaint from Jane. She went on to become a staff member at the hospital, an associate professor at McGill University, a fellow of the Royal College of Physicians and Surgeons of Canada, and the first blind physician to qualify as a specialist in internal medicine.

As I watched her work, it was hard to believe how Jane's optimism seemed to inspire a deeper humanity within her colleagues wherever she was assigned. Among always-busy residents, no one was ever too busy to be avail-

*Written with the consent of Jane Poulson.

able to Jane for whatever she might require. Her fellow residents recorded chapters of medical texts and journal articles (sometimes with unsolicited commentary) onto her ubiquitous audiocassette tapes. Her patients, initially uncertain about this blind doctor, quickly understood that her appreciation of their illnesses and her handling of their cases was, in fact, *better* than they had ever had before.

Within the Montreal General, our pride in Jane was palpable. She did her medical training with us, began her career with us in internal medicine, and participated in the hospital's program of palliative care. Her patient care and the inspirational way she taught students and residents became legendary.

In the 1990s, Jane felt that she should be closer to her family in Toronto, and so with heavy hearts we said goodbye and good luck as she continued her career down the 401. Shortly after her move, Jane suffered a myocardial infarction. To everyone's great relief, she underwent successful coronary bypass surgery. As if this wasn't enough, Jane was then diagnosed with breast cancer and underwent surgery, chemotherapy, and radiation therapy.

Throughout these tribulations, her resilience, optimism, and indomitable spirit never dimmed. In 1998 in the *Canadian Medical Association Journal*, she wrote of her experience: "None of the conditions I have lived with—not juvenile diabetes, not blindness, not heart disease—has had the emotional impact of cancer." Her unique perspective as a physician–patient with a disability made her next essay, published in *The New England Journal of Medicine*, a similarly invaluable contribution. There, she describes the psychological injury and worry that doctors unwittingly inflict on their patients when they say things like "Our newer technologies are so much better," or "Don't worry—your hair will grow back," or "You're not eligible for this study," or even, overheard talking with another physician, "I have a really great case"—when that case is you.

Thinking of Jane, I have often been reminded of the biblical Book of Job and its story of a man of great faith who is beset by trials and tribulations due to a celestial wager. In the midst of his suffering, Job is visited by three friends, presumably healers, who rather than comfort him spend their time accusing him of the sins for which he is supposedly being punished. Job eventually admonishes his physicians: "No doubt but that ye are the people and wisdom shall die with you" and, more to the point, "Miserable comforters are ye all."

Jane Poulson passed away in 2001, but her legacy of faith, courage, and insight remain in her autobiography *The Doctor Will Not See You Now*—the black humour in the title is so much Jane—and in the memory she left with family and colleagues.

Don't bring cold comfort, she reminds us. Never give up hope. It's no wonder that for her unprecedented accomplishments, Jane Poulson was made a member of the Order of Canada.

Me with my cameras. I used to take pictures everywhere I went, and did for many years.

Rubber Chicken Dinners

Every profession creates its own community, and biomedicine is no exception. After the initial discovery of CEA, I was soon flooded with requests to present papers, attend symposia, join associations, sit on grant committees, and on and on. The peripatetic aspect of my life began.

Evelyn, to her great credit, never complained about all the travel my career required. Most of it was short-hop stuff, one or two nights away, trips on which she sometimes came along, sitting beside me through endless after-dinner speeches and "rubber chicken dinners," as she jokingly called them. There were so many events like this, in fact, Ev kept a log of them. Here are a few stories from the road.

Burroughs Wellcome Fund

For half a dozen years I sat on the board of the Burroughs Wellcome Fund, and every three months I spent a few days in Durham, NC, meeting a shortlist of outstanding young scientists in biomedicine whose research the board considered supporting. This arrangement was almost unique, in that most funding organizations do not see applicants in the flesh; but talking with them in person made a real difference to our understanding of their work.

Evelyn does not love flying. But she loved attending the annual gathering of the Burroughs Wellcome Fund board, which happened away from its head office in warm locales like Los Angeles, San Diego, and Florida. My Burroughs colleagues—superb scientists like Enriqueta (Queta) Bond (board president), Carlos Bustamante, Gail Cassell, Jerome Strauss, George

Miller, Judith Swain, and others—all looked forward to seeing Ev, whose good humour, wit, and sensitivity always made her a hit. Indeed, I sometimes thought the others kept me on the board just so they could have an annual talk with her!

ISOBM

In 1973, Hidematsu Hirai and I and a few others formed the International Society of Oncology and Biomarkers (ISOBM) to help researchers in our brand-new field share findings and coordinate activities. (The society's journal is the excitingly named *Tumor Biology*.) ISOBM meetings were great fun, especially when Evelyn came along, and we got to see a lot of the world and reconnect with professional friends and acquaintances, who often brought their spouses as well. We became good friends with Garri Abelev in Russia, Sabine von Kleist in Germany, Hidematsu Hirai and Kohzoh Imai in Japan, Sten Hammerstrom and Torgny Stigbrand in Sweden, Jean-Pierre Mach in Switzerland, Jose Uriel in France, Vivian Barak in Israel, Markku Seppala in Finland, Alexander Munro Neville in England, and Bill Fishman, Herb Kupchik, David Goldenberg, Erkki Ruoslahti, John Shively, and Stewart Sell, among others, in the United States. Evelyn called ISOBM the "Travelling Club" for good reason: over the years, we held meetings in all the countries mentioned above.

One scientist, Garri Abelev, merits further mention. In 1976, he and I had the pleasure of sharing ISOBM's first Outstanding Achievement Award (now the Abbott Award). In the 1960s, Garri had successfully described alpha-fetoprotein, long known to be produced by the fetal liver, as a product of liver cancer as well. He regularly travelled around the world to share findings and visit patients, especially in Africa, where liver cancer was rampant. He did so until the early 1970s, when the Soviet government asked him to act as a clandestine government agent during his visits to other countries. His ethical principles prohibited him from accepting such an assignment—but he knew there would be consequences. At a conference in Quebec City, he asked me to follow him into the bathroom. "Garri, what's up?" I asked. "Phil, you won't see me for a couple of years," he said. "Please send me journals whenever you can, and I will send you a postcard every Christmas to let you know I am still alive." For the next half-dozen years, Garri wasn't permitted to travel abroad and his Moscow laboratory was shut down. Being Jewish in the USSR was not an advantage for him either. During those years I mailed scientific journals to his home address, to help him keep abreast of the field, and every Christmas I got a card that always read, "I am fine. Have a happy holiday." Then in 1980, I and other ISOBM members decided to boycott our annual conference, to be held in Tallin, and told the Soviet Academy of Sciences that we would not travel to the Soviet Union for any scientific purpose until Abelev was reinstated and allowed to travel outside the USSR. Soon after, he appeared at ISOBM

LEFT: Snorkelling in the Caribbean.

RIGHT: Ev and I on holiday after a medical conference in Jerusalem. During my tenure as physician-in-chief, Ev became a crucial volunteer in my office and in some ways got to know the staff and residents better than I did, since she had time to listen to people's problems and would pass on the significant ones to me at dinner. Our working holidays were a welcome change of pace and something of a reward for both of us.

meetings in Europe and Canada. Garri credited much of his release from Soviet restrictions to this strong support within ISOBM.

The Aged Plaque

On a number of occasions, Michael Sela invited me to lecture at the Weizmann Institute in Rehovot, Israel. Michael was president of the Weizmann, of which he was rightfully proud, and on one visit he encouraged me to stay on as his guest for a few days.

"And do bring your lovely wife," he added. They had met at another meeting.

When I arrived at his office from the airport, Michael was shouting into the phone in rapid Hebrew. He hung up, composed himself, and greeted me. I asked if there was a serious problem. It turned out that Mrs. Geshtetner, of Geshtetner photocopier fame, was coming that afternoon to officially open a building funded by her family and named in her husband's memory. The building had actually been open for several years by then, but unfortunately, due to an oversight, no one had put up the requisite dedicatory plaque on the front of the building. The "shop" could produce a plaque quickly—but its shiny newness, which would be obvious to all, might cause major offence.

"Don't worry," said Michael, "as we speak, they are aging it appropriately."

An hour or so later, Michael was called to the ceremony. I tagged along. To my astonishment, a large, well-polished, venerable-looking plaque was already installed beside the front door, looking as if it had been there for years. Michael turned lovingly to the plaque, spoke of the Geshtetners' enduring support, and made a fine speech.

In the evening, Evelyn and I accompanied Michael to dinner, where we met Mrs. Geshtetner and Ruth Arnon, a Weizmann professor and international scientific star. Michael insisted that everyone taste his soup, using only one spoon. Evelyn, sitting next to Michael, was the first to have the pleasure and, as a good guest, agreed the soup was wonderful. Michael was a superb and gregarious host.

"As long as you're in Israel, anything you need, let me know," he said.

"Thank you, Michael," I said. "For my first request, I would ask that you take your hands off my wife."

The rest of the evening was great.

Find the Pea: Christmas Dinner with Monique Bégin

Life often takes us in strange directions, and one such episode for me involved politician Monique Bégin. Bégin was one of the first three women ever elected to the House of Commons, and she and I met when she was Minister of Health and Welfare for the Trudeau Liberals (1980–84). In my role as physician-in-chief at the General, I invited her to give a lecture at Grand Medical Rounds and outline her plans for supporting medical research. She accepted, gave a terrific talk, and we became good acquaintances.

A few years later, after she had left politics and joined the University of Ottawa, Monique invited Ev and me to a Christmas dinner party at her home in Cartierville. After arriving and receiving a warm welcome from our hostess, we went in to find a number of acquaintances from the medical, research, and political communities. Indeed, there was even a colleague from McGill there with his rather overbearing and terribly proper wife, who was very bright but had little people sense.

After chatter and dinner, everyone was given a small muffin, randomly, and informed that in two of the muffins there would be a pea, one for the men and one for the women. The two lucky pea-recipients would then be named King and Queen of the Night. Ev said to me, sotto voce, that if she got the pea she was going to swallow it, and suggested I do the same. And so the game proceeded. We ate our muffins. Ev and I smiled at each other. Safe! But G-d is good, and the rather overbearing wife of the colleague mentioned above had found the pea! She and the king were then seated on an elevated platform in the middle of the living room while the rest of us danced around the platform, clapping and singing to music.

"That was worth the price of admission," said Evelyn on the way home. "Tonight was definitely *not* a rubber chicken dinner."

Dinner with the Prime Minister

Brian Mulroney was prime minister from 1984 to 1993. At some point in 1984, his wife, Mila, decided to do a Jackie Kennedy and started hosting dinner parties at 24 Sussex Drive for Canadians from diverse walks of life.

Anthony Jenkins' cartoon from *The Globe and Mail*, September 8, 1984, after dinner with the Mulroneys. Jenkins has me as a geeky beaver in bowtie and running shoes, next to a very self-assured prime minister with a chin the size of Greenland.

As a member of the Medical Research Council (MRC), I had met Mila through her fundraising efforts for cystic fibrosis and was duly invited to attend one such evening.

On a drizzly night, Ev and I turned up, a bit damp, at the prime minister's residence. Brian was greeting guests in the foyer.

"Ah, we're safe now, the doctor's here," he said with a grin.

"If you want it to stay that way, you'd best make sure the Medical Research Council is better funded," I replied, only half-joking.

"Michael, is there a problem there?" he said, turning to Michael Wilson, the Minister of Finance, who was standing next to him.

"Uh, ask Jake," said Wilson, referring to Jake Epp, the Minister of Health.

As I later learned, the Minister of Health didn't even know the MRC was in his portfolio. His greatest concern that evening was an upcoming live roundtable discussion on CBC, specifically the possibility that his Mennonite father might see him on television discussing the use of condoms for safe sex.

At dinner, there were two tables of eight. I was seated at Brian Mulroney's table between political cartoonist Anthony Jenkins and artist Molly Lamb.

Evelyn was at the other table beside artist Bruno Bobak (Molly's husband) and news anchor Lloyd Robertson, who was much shorter than he appeared on television.

"I had to buy two thrift-shop tuxedos for this event," Bobak whispered to Ev. "Only the pants fit from the first suit, and only the jacket from the second."

As the evening progressed, Brian tapped his glass and stood up to make a toast.

"Mila and I are delighted to have our dearest friends with us here tonight," he began.

"If that's the case, he's really in trouble," I whispered to my dinner mates. The next morning a lovely cartoon by Jenkins appeared in *The Globe and Mail*, showing a beaverish physician on a couch beside a self-assured prime minister with a chin the size of Greenland.

As 10 p.m. rolled around, someone at our table whispered to the group: "When they say the evening ends at ten, what they really mean is, Out the door by ten."

We made our way to our waiting car and were, happily, driven back to Montreal.

Teaching: The Eyes Have It

Upon becoming a clinician-scientist, teaching became a regular and much-loved activity of mine.

The first time I "taught" was in grade five at Bancroft Elementary. Miss Lieffer asked if I would like to lead the class through our history and geography lessons, so I spent the next few evenings going over the material I was to cover. But as I looked at the fact sheet I had developed, it struck me that I would lose my classmates' attention if all I did was spew facts at them. And so I tried to tell a story instead, using the facts as guideposts. In history, the story is about people; in geography, it's about a place.

A few mornings later, as I spoke to the class, I searched their faces to see if I was getting through and found myself focusing on their eyes. And I used a phrase that I've kept using to this day: "Are we okay so far? Any questions?" I got nods and smiles from my friends, and a few questions. That outing was apparently a success.

Ten years later, during my fourth year of honours physiology at McGill, I spoke to the first-year medical students about a lab experiment they were about to do. I said my piece, but felt uncomfortable, and later realized why: on the greatly raised lectern, I was looking down on the heads of the assembled and so couldn't see their eyes. Without that feedback, I felt slightly lost.

Nowadays, teaching groups of five or six hundred, I always pick out three or four nearby, in the front rows, so I can watch their faces and see their reactions.

"Are we okay so far?" I say. "Any questions?"

What I learned in grade five still applies: the eyes have it.

All That Jazz

During my fifteen years as physician-in-chief, part of my job, as I saw it, was to get to know the residents, that is, the new young doctors doing their training on the wards of the General. Along with making them feel at home in the hospital, I enjoyed getting to know the future face of medicine in Canada and developing a sense of who among them might be ready to join us on staff. The manner of doing this was to "round" with the residents, visiting each of the medical wards for an hour, four times a week. One of the residents would present a case in the conference room on the ward, which the entire team then discussed, determining if anything had been omitted or should still be added to help determine diagnosis. Part of the experience, for residents, was also seeing how quickly I could make a diagnosis based on the information provided.

After a while, the chief resident's gathering cry to the staff to start rounds was, "It's showtime, folks"—the opening words of the movie *All That Jazz*. By the early 1980s, many people had seen the popular film, about the life and obsessions of dancer-choreographer Bob Fosse, and everyone got the joke. Evelyn and I had seen it when it came out. What I had assumed would be a nice, fairly tame musical turned out to be two hours of sex, drugs, alcohol, and an eerily familiar portrait of overcommitment to a career.

I loved it, especially the snapping fingers. And so four mornings a week, my visits with the residents always opened with a big grin and "It's showtime, folks."

The Gold Rounds

In their second year of medical school, students at McGill take "Introduction to Clinical Medicine," a course that involves examining patients on hospital wards. For students used to textbooks and lecture halls, learning on their feet with real patients can be a major change. To help them adapt, I would sit down with about twenty students, in a hospital conference room every Tuesday morning, in what came to be known as "Gold Rounds."

In these sessions, three students presented the real case of a flesh-and-blood patient whom they had examined the previous week on the wards of the General. They got the patient's case history, performed a physical examination, and made note of any tests that had been done.

Gold Rounds at the Montreal General, 1981. Learning how to examine and diagnose patients is not easy. Every Tuesday morning I would sit down with a group of second-year medical students and help them chart their course out of textbooks and into the lives of real sufferers.

Presenter 1 role-played the patient, Presenter 2 reported the results of the physical examination, and Presenter 3 reported on blood work and other tests, when asked by the other students. To start the session, the rest of the group asked questions in order, around the table, to obtain as complete a medical history as possible. The idea was for each student to formulate the best possible question, based on what they had already heard, and then justify the reasoning behind their own question. Why did they ask the question and what had they learned from the answer? In what direction were they heading? As questions were answered, the pool of information grew—sometimes in unexpected ways. Students had to listen very carefully if they wanted to craft a relevant question when their turn came.

The idea, of course, was to start them down the road to recognizing disease complexes. By the end of this process, a reasonable diagnosis was usually forthcoming. As the spring semester progressed, I could recognize those students who were fastest at seeing the direction in which a diagnosis was unfolding. These students gave me the greatest satisfaction, but there were many others who acquired the skill more slowly who would also be fine physicians.

By the end of these training sessions, students had grasped in as real a way as possible the principle espoused by Sir William Osler: "Listen to your patient; he is telling you the diagnosis."

Sometimes a patient's history took us in directions no one could have anticipated.

As an example, one patient selected for these sessions in the early 1990s was a young woman with Graves' disease, or an overactive thyroid gland. Her condition had been correctly diagnosed and she had been correctly

Sir William Osler posing for a photo in Edward Jenner's chair, Oxford University, 1905. "Listen to your patient," said Osler, "he is telling you the diagnosis."

treated for it. But while hearing her medical history, we also learned that she had dropped out of high school, run away from home, developed an expensive drug habit, and was supporting herself and her habit through prostitution.

"Well," I said to the group with a deep sigh, wrapping up our session, "we can pat ourselves on the back for treating her Graves' disease. But what have we done for her *life*?"

Our session ended there, but the students were clearly listening, and to my amazement and delight, six of them took my words as a challenge.

In some fashion to which I was never privy, they befriended the young woman while she was still in the hospital and convinced her to clean herself up. Kicking a drug habit is no easy task. But she did it. The students then convinced her to return to high school. But there was a problem: the young woman's pimp wouldn't allow it, and he was threatening her physically. The students didn't know how to make that stop.

At this point they came to me for help, and I learned of their incredible efforts and success. Honestly, I don't know what they expected me to do: I was a physician, not a hit man. But from my childhood growing up on the Main I was still acquainted with "a man who knew a man" who could convince the pimp to leave her alone. I never discussed the how or where or why with my students, but the matter was settled.

And here is where the story blossoms even more unexpectedly. Not only did the young woman graduate from high school, she completed CEGEP and an undergraduate degree at Concordia University as well. When I heard she was interested in law school, knowing she would not be able to share her backstory openly on her application, I quietly shared it with a few colleagues at McGill's law school, who saw her stellar academic record and decided to take a chance on her. She graduated in the top-ten percentile of her class and now practises family law in a moderately sized city in Quebec. Whenever she passes through Montreal, she and I have coffee in the hospital tuck shop.

This is one of the few times in my career I've helped my students to cure not just a disease but a life.

Medicine doesn't stop when a patient walks out the office, the clinic, or the hospital door. It continues into the community of which we are a part, and on which we, as doctors, must never turn our backs.

A Good Death

What is a good death?

The Hippocratic Oath, which doctors still take in a modified form, lacks one line, also attributed to Hippocrates: *Primum non nocere*, or *First, do no harm*. The implication, of course, is that it is a doctor's job to do everything in their power to take care of patients and make them better, without taking risks.

But death comes for all of us, and so there are many times when a patient's life cannot be saved, and the physician loses the battle. But there are different ways of losing. And some of them can be strangely positive.

One gentleman who comes to mind in this regard was a patient originally from India whom I knew when I was a resident in the late 1960s. His forebears had been farmers, and he had worked the soil as a boy before shifting his direction, remarkably, to become an entrepreneur in his native country, then emigrating to Canada and establishing a successful business in Montreal.

After a number of previous hospitalizations, his cancerous disease had reached a terminal stage, and there was nothing more to be done. He and his family were aware of this. When I would see him on my rounds, or drop by to chat occasionally, he often said he didn't like the idea of dying in bed.

"One should die close to the soil," he would say.

And so, on a warm summer night, it became obvious that he would not make it through to the next day. With the help of the head night nurse and an orderly, we put him on a gurney, wheeled him outside, and then moved him onto a blanket on the grass.

No doubt we were breaking a dozen hospital rules. I sat with him, his wife, and their two sons until dawn. And then, as if we were in a movie directed by Steven Spielberg, the sun rose and the man died. He died as he wished, close to the soil. I've never forgotten him, or that moment.

A good death is different for everyone. Our contract with life is, after all, a rental contract, and we don't get to write the terms. The medical profession may be nothing more than a sophisticated delaying of our inevitable eviction, but we have proven ourselves surprisingly ingenious, as a species, at delaying the inevitable. When the moment comes, modern medicine has placed a good death within the reach of more people—millions more—than ever before. As John Donne said of Death, if we cannot outpace him, at least we can make him run. These days he's running harder than ever.

White Coat Ceremony

The white coat ceremony is a medical-school ritual that marks students' transition from preclinical to clinical study. At McGill, the ceremony takes place toward the middle of the second year and involves a formal donning of the white coat. On one occasion, I spoke to the assembled sophomores. Here are excerpts from that address.

I'm truly delighted to address this very important gathering.

Everyone in this room has played a role in making this ceremony possible.

This starts with you, our students, of course, but includes your parents, friends, and teachers. Today is probably the day your parents will forgive all the angst you caused them as teenagers. We are all proud of you as you reach this turning point in your medical education and move on from the theoretical to the practical aspects of patient care.

Today you don the healer's habit, or white coat. In the old sense of the word, a "habit" sounds more appropriate for a religious order. But the term is equally valid for physicians, for like its religious counterpart, the medical profession is a calling to do good.

In fact, the white coat symbolizes a habit of behaviour, meaning, something we do spontaneously and repeatedly on a daily basis. Habits become our way of life.

So how did you get to be here?

Despite the uniqueness of each of you, three things determine all of our lives: genes, environment, and luck.

First, genes. Many donors are here today—your mothers and fathers—but also the countless generations who preceded them are also in the room, representing the cells needed to construct the genome that you carry and will likely pass along.

Second, environment. Modern science has shown us that genomic expression can be altered by a gene's environment, or epigenome, without a change in gene structure. Everything we've eaten, drunk, and breathed, all the emotions we've been exposed to over the course of our lives, shape our epigenome. And since we now know that epigenes transmit information trans-generationally, the epigenome also likely includes the experiences of our forebears.

The third determining factor in our lives is, of course, luck. To be consistent, I've coined the term *fortunome.* The fortunome represents the sum of people who have guided us toward our present destinies. In Tennyson's words, "I am part of all that I have met." As with genome and epigenome, the fortunome is different for each of us. But we each know the people who have shaped our own lives, for better or worse.

So much for genome, epigenome, and fortunome.

Now that you've chosen to be doctors, what should you do? Put another way, what do we physicians, handing out the white coats, want of you?

Nothing more than this: we want you to become very good, perhaps even great, doctors.

Our wish is not entirely altruistic. The older my colleagues and I get, the more the plaintive cry is raised, Who will look after us? The answer, of course, is that you will. Doctors have been asking this question for centuries, and the answer is always the same.

Teach your children well.

In 1657, physician William Harvey said the workings of the human body are "hardly perceived unless we are deprived of them or they become deranged in some way." As I then tell my students, using the image above, Joni Mitchell said something similar in 1970, in "Big Yellow Taxi": "Don't it always seem to go that you don't know what you've got 'til it's gone?"

Gold's Rules for Medical Students

The Danish philosopher Kierkegaard said, "Life can only be understood backwards; but it must be lived forwards."

This is, in many ways, the perfect description of a medical education. Our task as doctors, of course, is not to do anything that may harm the patient, going forward. But the key to this is gaining knowledge of a patients' medical history, going backwards.

With this spirit in mind, I've come up with ten rules.

Not the Golden Rules, not the Ten Commandments—just ten suggestions for medical students. Gold's Rules.

Rule 1. You're Never Alone

There will always be those to whom you can turn for help, regardless of where you are in your career. There are few days when a good doctor, assessing patients, does not seek the opinion of colleagues with a deeper knowledge in specific areas. It doesn't matter whether they are students who are more senior than you, residents, the staff rounder, or the chief of service. When you are uncertain of what to do, don't hesitate to get help—even at three o'clock in the morning. An awakened doctor may be grumpy in the moment, but they'll be a lot less happy on rounds the next day if you haven't called.

Rule 2. You're Not a Fifth Wheel

It is normal for second-year medical students to feel like they don't belong. Senior students, residents, staff doctors, and consulting specialists have already seen the patient. What are *you* doing there? The answer is simple: we forfeit the right to call ourselves academic medical centres without your presence on the wards. Without you, I'm out of a job. Not good. So you are due the respect of any other medical professional.

Rule 3. Ask Stupid Questions

Don't be embarrassed if you don't understand a concept. Chances are, many of your classmates feel the same— and they won't ask either. Perhaps your key contribution to academia at this time in your careers is to ask why! Without this subtle, repeated push for answers, your mentors may forget the reasons and go through the motions without a great deal of thought. The only truly stupid question is the one you don't ask.

Rule 4. Don't Scare Patients

Most patients grow bored through long days of illness and recovery in hospital. So when you approach someone and say, "My name is Jane Smith, I'm a second-year medical student and I was hoping to examine you," they will

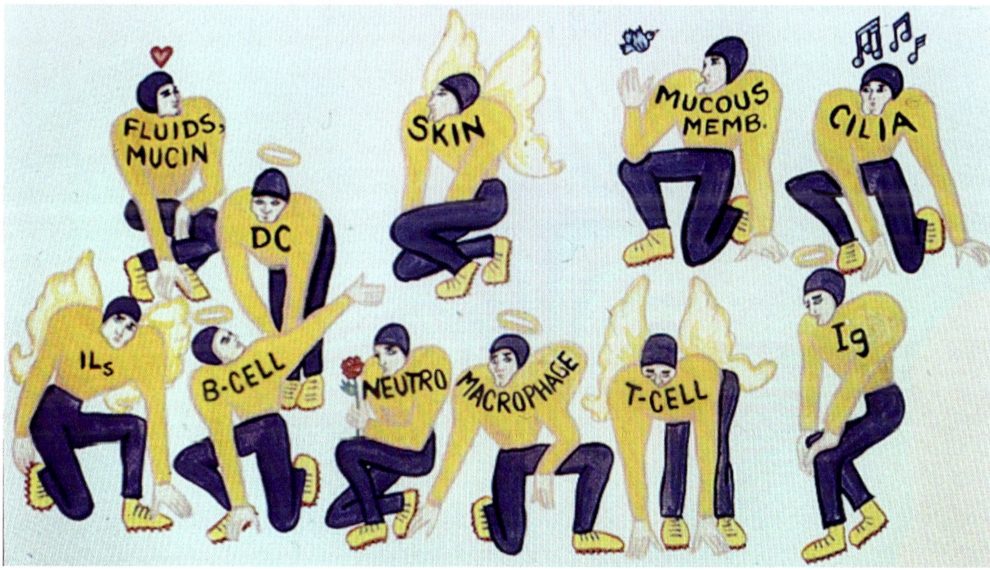

Slides from one of my immunology lectures. I use metaphors whenever I can, and students always seem to remember these slides best.

probably say yes just to break up the boredom. Now, you know you're a student, and they know you're a student—you've just told them—but the moment the examination begins, in the eyes of many patients you suddenly become a fully licensed physician with thirty years' experience. Your every move, sound, and facial gesture is no longer yours. What would be a normal expression of surprise or concern among friends now seems dramatic, to the patient, perhaps a sign they have a disease that none of the actual doctors who's examined them has previously noticed. So if a patient answers your questions in unexpected ways, don't wrinkle your forehead and exclaim,

"Oh!" Instead, just nod and say, "Uh-huh" in an even tone. Part of your medical training, in other words, is learning the mannerisms of the profession you hope to join.

Rule 5. Visit Patients Again
Many patients have few visitors, and your repeated presence can do wonders for them psychologically—which is a large part of the healing process. Doing so will also allow you to follow the course of the disease. In fact, you will probably have more time to do this as a medical student than at any time in your future career.

Rule 6. Listen, Think, then *Act*
Most doctors don't like to admit that they have a listening problem. In *How Doctors Think*, Jerome Groopman reports that the average time a patient gets to speak about their medical issues, before the doctor interrupts them, is about seventeen seconds. You can't learn much in seventeen seconds. "Listen to your patient," wrote Sir William Osler, an erstwhile McGillian, "he is telling you the diagnosis."

Rule 7. Learn from Each Patient
The first patient you see with any condition is the one who remains in your mind's eye—a shadowy figure that represents all your previous experience of patients suffering from that problem. But with every new patient, you will learn how a particular individual, perhaps even a culture, looks upon a disease process. When you learn how to learn, the knowledge of your patients will join that of your classmates and colleagues to enrich and guide you. My students have always been an enormous source of learning for me.

Rule 8. Never Remove Hope
No matter how bleak a situation may appear, the patient must be left with the sense that everything is being done to alleviate their pain or palliate their condition. Never lie to your patients about the severity of their problem. But always leave on the light of hope before you leave the room.

Rule 9. Always Provide Comfort
Sympathy for a fellow human being, letting them know you are sorry for their suffering, is the best medicine I know of which can be administered through the ear. Simple, effective remedies don't stop there: holding a patient's hand is also good medicine. Compassion is hopefully one of the reasons that you're in medical school today. Don't be afraid to use it.

Rule 10. Practise Menschlichkeit

This is the most important rule of all. *Menschlichkeit* is a German word adopted into many other languages. To be a mensch means, literally, to be a person. But the term means so much more than that. More than simply being a mensch or a stand-up person, *menschlichkeit* means to manifest humanity. Medical school's highest aim, beyond the learning of standards and procedures, is to turn students into carriers of that humanity. For the true medical mensch, altruism, compassion, and commitment guide their actions.

EKJ
25

PART VI

Mann tracht, Gott lacht

Clowns

More and more, over the course of my long career, I was surrounded by clowns.

OPPOSITE: Send in the clowns? Don't bother, they're here. A choice example from my collection.

Not the human type, but lovely miniatures in porcelain, glass, and other materials. They sat on shelves in my office and beside my desk and, depending on a visitor's age and experience, inspired discomfort, befuddlement, or amusement. Sometimes after learning of my strange collection, visitors even liked to add to it, bringing me figurines from far-flung places as well as the occasional strange clown painting. I've collected them for decades, and for a long time I had no idea *why* my habit began. But then in the leadup to my forty-fifth Baron Byng High School Reunion in 1998, I understood why.

Frances Kaufman, a high-school classmate, had asked me to serve as master of ceremonies for the event. She assured me I would only need to attend the final planning meeting. I was late for the meeting, uncharacteristically: I dragged my heels into the shower, I couldn't decide what to wear, my palms were sweaty in the taxi across town, and I was sure I was coming down with a terrible virus (I wasn't—even doctors can have hypochondriacal moments!).

At the meeting, sharing the story of my flustered feelings, many of my old classmates nodded in recognition. They had felt the same way before earlier meetings.

And, so, we come to the clowns.

It struck me very forcefully that the people around me in the room were the last ones who had seen me naked. Not literally naked, but something much more revealing: without a façade. As adults we learn how to reveal only certain parts of ourselves, depending on the situation, and to protect the rest. The clown is all façade: painted smile, comical frown, puffy pants,

(Man plans, G-d laughs)

ABOVE: I was surrounded by clowns at the Montreal General.

OPPOSITE: More clowns! People just kept bringing them to me. I'm thinking of donating them to the Children's Hospital.

flowery hat. We like the clown's exaggerated features, the sadness just behind the paint, and sometimes see ourselves in his pathos. But unlike the clown, over the course of our adult lives we forget that we're performing. The event reminded me of that fact. A high-school reunion is one of the few times as adults when our masks are useless.

With that revelation—at least to me—I've never looked at my clown collection the same way again. They don't frighten me, but perhaps it's this unexpected dichotomy that also makes clowns scary. That and the crazy makeup!

Baron Byng, Sixty-Five Years Later

Over Canadian Thanksgiving 2018, my classmates and I celebrated our sixty-fifth Baron Byng High School reunion with a brunch at Ruby Foo's Restaurant. Mort Levy, Sheila Pearl, Frances Kaufman, and I did the organizing that year.

Were we ever really this young? A social at the old Y on Mount Royal. I am in the middle row with Barbara Schwartz, and bottom left is Mort Levy (glasses) with Lila Klinger.

As the saying goes, *Mann tracht, Gott lacht*: Man plans, G-d laughs.

It had to be a brunch, as Frances explained to me, "because no one our age drives well in the dark or goes out late anymore." It had to be a restaurant with a lot of free parking. It had to be affordable: anything over $50/person might strain monthly budgets. Most importantly, there had to be no stairs. We also decided on a fifteen-minute limit for the Organ Recital—talk of dysfunctional organs—or we would be there all evening.

Then we did an informal rollcall of our former classmates:

"How about…?"

"Gone, I'm afraid."

"And…?"

"Alzheimer's."

"What about…"

"In terminal care."

"And…"

"In a golden-age facility."

"Can't get around anymore."

"Looking after her aging spouse."

We divided the remaining names of those we felt were still able to attend.

Reconvening a week later, we reported the sad facts. Many classmates we had considered viable candidates were either no longer with us or simply unable to get around. Mort seemed to have gotten a particularly difficult list. "If I ever suggest something like this again, stop me somehow," he said.

When reunion day came, we still had a great time. And some old friends who had moved farther afield, to places like California and Florida, made their way home.

Roddick Gates, McGill, painting by Terry Tomalty

We were the blessed ones, sitting there in apparently decent health, bursting with *nachas* for our grandchildren, some still driving (even at night), some still able to negotiate stairwells. But still, I couldn't avoid the thought of what awaits us, not too far down the road.

Coda: The Roddick Gates

In September 2019, sixty-six years after Mort Levy and I entered McGill, the two of us walked back through the Roddick Gates together.

These days, the gates are kept open virtually all of the time.

Mort had just retired in the summer. In a few months, the COVID-19 pandemic would arrive, during which I, too, would end my daily practice at the hospital, leaving only teaching still on my plate.

"You know, I think we've left this place better than we found it," I said.

Mort, being Mort, shrugged.

And then we met our wives for dinner.

Dr. Phil Gold, by Max Stiebel, MGH Foundation. The painting hangs on the 6th floor (the main entrance from Cedar Avenue) in the General.

Afterword

The following profile was commissioned by the McGill Department of Medicine and originally appeared in its 2020 Annual Report. My thanks to Dr. Marc Rodger and McGill University for permission to reprint it here.

The Ride of a Lifetime
by Ashley Rabinovitch

As Dr. Phil Gold prepares to retire from McGill University after six decades of service, his friends and colleagues paint a vivid portrait of an icon whose influence will be felt for generations to come.

In the fall of 1953, Dr. Phil Gold set foot on campus for the very first time. As he surveyed the stately porticos, the fresh-cut lawns, and the sea of unfamiliar faces, he turned to his best friend, Mortimer Levy, and said, "Mort, I'm going to leave this place better than I found it."

And he did.

Over the next six decades, Dr. Gold's accomplishments in cancer and immunology research, clinical practice, hospital administration, and teaching would become the stuff of legend. Now, at the age of 83, he has accumulated more letters than the alphabet behind his name and more awards and accolades than he can list from memory.

It would have been easy for someone who made a once-in-a-lifetime research breakthrough at 29 years old to rest on his laurels. Dr. Gold could easily have become arrogant or detached, content to inhabit an upper echelon of intellectual superstars without much concern for the everyday concerns of his patients, colleagues, or students. But that's not what happened.

Finding the needle in a haystack

As an undergraduate student in Honours Physiology at McGill, Dr. Gold never harboured any aspirations to attend medical school. "Frankly, I saw medicine as a distraction," he admits. "I was much more interested in pursuing a career in research at the time." Recognizing his potential, his mentor, Arnold Burgen, cajoled him into submitting an application, and the rest, as they say, is history.

Dr. Gold enjoyed medical school more than he anticipated and graduated with a handful of prizes to show for his academic achievements. After graduation, he began what would become a lifelong love affair with the Montreal General Hospital, an integral part of the McGill University Health Centre (MUHC). As the Montreal General celebrates 200 years, it's hard to overstate the impact of Dr. Gold on the past 50.

Back in 1961, though, he was a first-year resident in internal medicine who was deeply grieved at the ravages of cancer. "I saw so many patients who were suffering, and all we were doing for them was filling them with toxic chemicals, radiation and hope," Dr. Gold remembers. "I thought there had to be some better way."

In 1963, Dr. Gold embarked on a PhD in physiology in the laboratory of Dr. Sam Freedman, a well-established clinical Allergist. His career trajectory shifted dramatically when he heard a lecture and then found a paper on immunologic tolerance. The paper's author had demonstrated that if researchers expose an animal to a foreign molecule in utero or immediately after birth, they can fool the animal's immune system into thinking that it's native to their body. The paper sparked an idea to induce tolerance to human normal bowel in a newborn rabbit. Dr. Gold's mentor, Sir Arnold Burgen, tried to dissuade him from pursuing it, insisting that "the field of cancer research is littered with the bodies of people with good ideas."

Dr. Gold's unusual experiment succeeded beyond anyone's wildest dreams. He successfully induced tolerance to a normal human bowel in newborn rabbits, injected them with human bowel cancer cells from the same donor, as adults, and searched for any difference in how the rabbits' immune systems reacted to cancer cells compared to normal cells. He found what they were looking for, and what he called: carcinoembryonic antigen (CEA), a protein that indicates the presence of cancer.

Once the word began to spread, Dr. Gold's career took flight. The paper he co-authored with Dr. Freedman was the most highly cited in the world at one point in time, and the FDA soon recognized CEA as the first human tumour marker for cancer. To this day, clinicians use a CEA blood test to diagnose and manage certain types of cancer, particularly cancers of the large intestine and rectum.

Dr. Gold frequently remarks that three things determine the course of one's life: "the genome, the epigenome, and the fortunome—in other words, your genes, your environment and luck." He designed an experiment in a way that removed the haystack to find the needle, and it worked. "I was lucky, and I knew I was lucky," he reflects. "I know me better than anyone knows me, and I'm not a genius."

His contemporaries beg to differ. According to Dr. Abraham Fuks, another renowned McGill immunologist who previously served as Dean of the Faculty of Medicine from 1995 to 2006, Dr. Gold achieved a rare feat. "Aside from the fact that he was so young when it happened, his findings were monumental when you consider their lasting impact," Dr. Fuks reflects. "Not many lab tests innovated in 1965 are still used clinically today. That's remarkable. This is what happens when highly ambitious, talented people find ways to execute a creative idea."

Dr. Richard Cruess, who preceded Dr. Fuks as Dean of the Faculty of Medicine from 1981 to 1995, was the attending orthopaedic surgeon at the Royal Victoria Hospital at the time of the discovery of CEA. "At that time, there was this feeling that wonderfully exciting things were happening in cancer immunology," says Dr. Cruess. "Along with Sam Freedman, Phil really did create a whole new world of possibility in cancer research. That's what makes him such an icon."

The grandfather of cancer research

If there is one thing that Dr. Gold regrets, it was the failure of the hospital and/or university to negotiate a royalty on profits from CEA testing, which could have generated much needed funding from which both organizations could have benefited.

Even without a windfall of cash, Dr. Gold and his colleagues leveraged the discovery of CEA to launch a new chapter in cancer research and clinical care at McGill. Dr. Fuks, who was a resident at the Montreal General at the time, still remembers the impression that Dr. Gold and his colleagues made on the people around them. "Phil Gold, Sam Freedman, Joe Shuster, and David Hawkins worked so well as a group and demonstrated so much joy in their work that they influenced my own decision to choose immunology as a clinical and research career," he affirms.

Dr. Gold and his research group relocated to the McIntyre Medical Sciences Building in 1976. He accepted the role as the first director of the newly inaugurated McGill Cancer Centre while serving as a professor of medicine and physiology at the Faculty of Medicine. The Centre evolved into the first university-based Department of Oncology in North America, which now includes the world-class Rosalind and Morris Goodman Cancer Centre.

"People like Dr. Gold saw the future," says Dr. David Eidelman, the current Dean of the Faculty of Medicine and Health Sciences. "Unlike most people of his time, he approached cancer as a subject of mechanistic inquiry instead of this mysterious, hopelessly untreatable disease."

The discovery of CEA has given rise to more than a few scientific careers over the decades. Dr. Nicole Beauchemin, a principal investigator at the Goodman Cancer Research Centre, calls herself the "scientific granddaughter" of Dr. Gold, with her mentor, Dr. Abe Fuks, in the generation above her. "Phil is like the root of a very large, majestic oak tree," she illustrates. "With the discovery of CEA, he opened up a new field of research and inspired dozens of research teams to build upon his work. Every year, the tree grows more branches."

In 1986, Dr. Beauchemin contributed her experience in molecular biology and cloning to a Cancer Centre project designed to successfully clone the CEA gene. She and other researchers, both in and out of the McGill ecosystem, went on to discover nearly 30 more genes that all relate in some way to the original CEA protein. By using these proteins as markers to track, treat, and understand cancer cells, they can develop targeted therapies to treat cancer based on gene expression profiles.

To Dr. Beauchemin, Dr. Gold is like a founding father whose footprints are visible everywhere she looks. "To this day, he still participates in meetings of the global CEA research community," she attests. "That passion for discovery and possibility has never waned."

If Dr. Beauchemin is a scientific granddaughter of Dr. Gold, Dr. Genèvieve Genest is a great-granddaughter. Initially inspired to enter the field of immunology after an electrifying presentation by Dr. Gold in her microbiology class, Dr. Genest is on track to become a clinician-researcher at the Montreal General. "He's served as a mentor figure from the beginning," she affirms. "He's the type of person to say, 'Look, kid, let me show you who and what you need to know.'" When Dr. Genest developed an interest in treating women with a history of unexplained recurrent miscarriages, Dr. Gold encouraged her to explore the linkages between fertility and immunology. Thanks to his encouragement, Dr. Genest has emerged as McGill's first reproductive immunologist.

Honey over vinegar

In 1980, Dr. Gold returned to the Montreal General as Physician-in-Chief and simultaneously served as the Chairman of the Department of Medicine at McGill University between 1985 and 1990. Dr. Christos Tsoukas, who has served as Director of the Division of Clinical Allergy and Immunology at the McGill University Health Centre (MUHC) since 2007, was a resident when Dr. Gold made his return. In those years, the Montreal General was "very much a reflection of the past," Dr. Tsoukas recalls. "Dr. Gold's predecessor ran the hospital like an army general. He was so intimidating that your knees would start to buckle whenever you ran into him."

When Dr. Gold took the helm, the atmosphere shifted perceptibly. "Dr. Gold would go out of his way to relate to residents with enthusiasm and collegiality, and that's an attitude that continues today through all of the directors and division leaders who were once residents," says Dr. Tsoukas.

Dr. Tsoukas highlights a truth that surprises many people who meet Dr. Gold for the first time: While he is often the most revered person in the room, he's also the kindest. "He's always shaking your hand or giving you a hug," says Dean Eidelman. "He has remarkably few enemies for someone at his level."

According to Dr. Tsoukas, Dr. Gold is someone who would be called an "influencer" in today's parlance, a cheerleader who rallies his team to greatness by setting an example. "He has always encouraged, not dictated, while maintaining a healthy sense of humour," says Dr. Tsoukas.

Dr. Tsoukas remembers the time when a visiting medical student from Greece was overwhelmed with excitement about meeting Dr. Gold, whose reputation had preceded him from across the globe. The student, who struggled to fully express himself in English, tried to tell Dr. Gold, "I want to be like you," but what came out instead was, "I would like to be in your shoes." With a twinkle in his eye, Dr. Gold immediately took off his shoes and offered them to the bewildered student.

While he rarely misses an opportunity to make someone laugh, Dr. Gold has also been known to convey quiet empathy in moments of crisis. Dr. Tsoukas will never forget the day he showed Dr. Gold a photo of his son, born prematurely at less than two pounds. "I can still picture the face he made when he looked at the photo," says Dr. Tsoukas. "It was pained but full of compassion. To have someone who is your superior relate like that to your struggles, along with your happiness, is rare and meaningful."

Dr. Gold has always maintained that people accomplish more with honey than with vinegar. "I genuinely enjoy being nice to people," he affirms. "And when you're nice to people, you find that they're frequently nice to you." But while kindness has always served him as a strategic asset, there is nothing calculating about his desire to make colleagues and patients feel seen and valued.

On one particularly memorable day, the condition of a terminal cancer patient at the Montreal General was declining quickly. The patient grew up on a farm in India, where people prefer to die as close to the land as possible. Dr. Gold fulfilled his patient's dying wish by wheeling him out to the hospital lawn, where he sat with his family members and caregivers for several hours as he took his final breaths. As the sun rose, he died on the ground, exactly where he wanted to die. Dr. Gold sat with him for four hours that day.

Untrammeled optimism

When Dr. Gold accepted the role as Physician-in-Chief at the Montreal General, he encountered a dire financial situation. "I went to the cupboard, and the cupboard was bare," he says. "We had no money to do what we need to do." At the next departmental meeting, he announced a plan for closing the gaps that involved mild cuts to clinical income for the staff, to which they agreed.

From Dr. Cruess's perspective, no one climbs to the top of the ladder without the ability to make unpopular decisions and endure high levels of stress. Dr. Gold has seemingly mastered the art of paddling furiously beneath the surface while maintaining a calm, jovial exterior. For years at a time, he chain smoked his way through long hours of reading and survived on four hours of sleep a night. Before taking over as Chair of the Department of Medicine at McGill, he re-read an entire textbook on internal medicine from cover to cover. "There is a lot of steel and ambition in him," Dr. Cruess has observed. "But it's all layered on top of this wonderful personality. Even the disagreements were fun."

What strikes people most when they work with Dr. Gold in any capacity is his "untrammeled optimism," says Dr. Fuks. "He has this can-do attitude combined with energy, and that makes him come across as larger than life. When you walk into a room, you know he's there." According to Dean Eidelman, "Uncle Phil," as he was known at the Montreal General, could be so unrelentingly optimistic that he came across as unrealistic at times. Even in the most bleak funding environments, Dr. Gold could be relied upon to focus on what could be done, not what couldn't be done. "He taught me that I have a significant ability to change my worldview if I choose to do so," says Dean Eidelman.

Ultimately, Dr. Gold's sunny outlook played an instrumental role in persuading donors to give generously and staff to economize willingly. By the time he stepped down in 1995 to become the Executive Director of the Clinical Research Centre at the MUHC, the cupboard was full.

Passing the baton

Despite his decades of accomplishment as a clinician-researcher, Dr. Gold places the greatest value on his teaching efforts. "Research is ultimately a shot in the dark," he reflects. "If you're lucky, as I was, you win. But teaching the next generation is how you reproduce yourself."

Dr. Fuks, who has written extensively on the power of metaphor in medical discourse and teaching, points to Dr. Gold's famous use of metaphors in his immunology lectures. Former students like Dr. Genest can still recall in detail the way Dr. Gold likes to equate the immune system with two football teams, assigning each player on the team a role. "Phil knows how to tell a story rather than putting facts onto a board," says Dr. Fuks.

Dr. Cruess, who once created a small group program to study professional identity formation, could always rely on Dr. Gold to light up a room with his quick wit and enthusiastic demeanor. "Phil in a small group with medical students is sheer magic," he has witnessed. "It's hard to get him out of the room."

Dr. Gold still teaches guest lectures when invited, but he is satisfied with the legacy he is leaving behind as he eases into retirement. "I'm not sure what else I would like to accomplish," he acknowledges. "My children and grandchildren have gone on to do great things, as have my former students. Whatever I wanted to accomplish in the lab is behind me. It's been the ride of a lifetime, and I'm grateful for it."

Lately, Dr. Gold has starting to think more about what happens going forward. "I've done the best that I could. Now I'll leave it to my colleagues and students to continue to break new ground, I look forward to watching that happen."

Acknowledgements

To Evelyn and my children and grandchildren: This book is for you. Each of you has helped to make my life a great pleasure.

To Mortimer Levy: To have a friend I can call on, without hesitation, who always has my best interests at heart, and who's there in good times and bad, is a gift I cherish. Since grade one at Bancroft Elementary, Mort, you've been that friend to me.

My working life has been linked to countless colleagues, students, and patients. The students to whom I've given lectures, including those whom I have mentored, number in the tens of thousands—indeed, many later became colleagues. My patients have numbered in the thousands. To try to name and thank them all would be a fool's errand. But there are a few colleagues and mentors to whom I will remain forever grateful and indebted: Sir Arnold Burgen, Dr. Richard Cruess, Dr. Samuel O. Freedman, and Dr. Joseph Shuster have been there for me at critical times in my life and career.

My thanks to friends and colleagues: Alan Barkun, Nicole Beauchemin, Abe Fuks, Genèvieve Genest, Laurence Green, Steven Grover, Tim Meagher, David Mulder, Chris Tsoukas, Blair Whittemore, and the late Harvey Barkun. They represent so many others, and their support and friendship has meant a great deal to me. Thanks also to our travelling friends Norman Zavalkoff and Gail Gold, Sandra and Larry Charney, and Rochelle and the late Norman Malus. We consider ourselves fortunate to have seen the world with such good friends.

I'd also like to give heartfelt thanks to my remarkable secretaries, most particularly Shelley Natovitch, who has seen me through the last years of my active career with daily kindness and indulgence. To Lianne Arbour, Anna Cuccovia, Anna Iacucci, Maria Orsini, and Penny Roumeliotis, my appreciation for your tolerance and support throughout my professional life. I beg forgiveness of those not mentioned.

Thank you to Herb Berkovitz, Margaret Suttie, the entire MGH200 team, and the MUHC Art & Heritage Centre for preserving the history of Montreal's hospitals, and the stories of its people, with such care. Thanks to the Canadian Medical Hall of Fame (CMHF) for assisting with some black-and-white images. Thanks to Kristian Gravenor for helping track down L'Échourie. Thanks to Ashley Rabinovitch for her wonderful profile, "The Ride of a Lifetime." And a special thank you to Jean-Guy Gourdeau, President of the MGH Foundation, for his timely and generous support of this book.

Thanks to Brian Morgan, for his superb book design, and to the good people at McGill-Queen's University Press, including executive director Philip Cercone, managing editor Kathleen Fraser, and publicist Jacqui Davis, who went above and beyond in their efforts to get this book into the public eye. And my sincere thanks to my editor, Derek Webster. Without Derek's input and ongoing encouragement, I doubt that this memoir would ever have been completed.

The family in Israel, 2013. Back row, from left: Natalie, Ian, Michael, Benji, Cleve, Josie, Zack, Ev, Alex (Django), me. Front row: Adam and Matthew. Not present for this photo: Joel and Amalia.

Timeline: Dr. Phil Gold

1942–49	Bancroft Elementary
1949–53	Baron Byng Secondary
1953–57	Bachelor of Science, Honours Physiology, McGill University
1957–61	Doctor of Medicine, Faculty of Medicine, McGill University
1961	Master of Science, Physiology, McGill University
1963	Initial studies of human tumour marker, leading to identification of carcinoembryonic antigen (CEA)
1965	First publications of CEA results in *Journal of Experimental Medicine*
1965	Ph.D., Physiology, McGill University
1972	Professor, Department of Medicine, McGill University (ongoing)
1974	Professor, Department of Physiology, McGill University (ongoing)
1976–80	Inaugural Director, McGill Cancer Centre
1976–80	Director, Division of Clinical Immunology and Allergy, Montreal General Hospital
1978	Johann-Georg-Zimmerman Prize for Cancer Research, Germany
1978	Gairdner Foundation Annual International Award
1979	Officer of the Order of Canada
1980–95	Physician-in-Chief, Montreal General Hospital
1982	Inaugural Ernest C. Manning Foundation Award
1983	St. Vincent Prize for Medical Research, Italy
1985	Isaak Walton Killam Award in Medicine of the Canada Council

1985–90	Chairman, Department of Medicine, McGill University
1985	*MacLean's* Magazine Most Outstanding Medical Personalities of the Past 25 Years
1986	Professor, Department of Oncology, McGill University (ongoing)
1986	Honorary Doctorate of Science, McMaster University
1986	Promoted to Companion of the Order of Canada
1986	Inducted into the Academy of Great Montrealers
1987	Douglas G. Cameron Professor of Medicine (ongoing)
1990	Officer of the Ordre National du Québec (Grand Officer, 2019)
1992	R.M. Taylor Medal, National Cancer Institute of Canada
1995	Executive Director, Clinical Research Centre, MUHC (ongoing)
1998	Named the Sir Arthur Sims Commonwealth Traveling Professor
2001	Honour List for Educational Excellence in Teaching, Faculty of Medicine, McGill University
2002	Queen Elizabeth II Jubilee Medal (Diamond Jubilee Medal, 2012)
2006	Inauguration of the Phil Gold Chair in Medicine, McGill University
2010	Elected to Canadian Medical Hall of Fame
2011	Lifetime Achievement Award, McGill University Health Centre (MUHC)
2012	Gerald Bronfman Center Lifetime Achievement Award, Department of Oncology, McGill
2013	Wilder-Penfield Prix du Québec
2015	Celebrations of 50th Anniversary of the First Publications on CEA: Zakopane, Poland (ISOBM conference), Montreal (McGill Symposium on CEA), and Washington, DC (International CEA Symposium)
2017	Inauguration, Phil Gold Distinguished Lectureship, Goodman Cancer Institute (GCI)
2017	Einstein Legacy Award, on the occasion of the centenary of the General Theory of Relativity
2022	Professor Emeritus, Faculty of Medicine, McGill University
2022	McGill University Medal for Exceptional Academic Achievement

TOP: Ev and I on our honeymoon in the Catskills, 1960. The night of our wedding we stayed at the Motel Raphael in Montreal (BOTTOM), because we wanted to get a good start on our drive south the next morning, and the motel was near the highway. So much for the Ritz!

TOP: A typical hospital pharmacy in Montreal, June 1944. Alongside the nurses is a nun from the order of the Daughters of Wisdom.

BOTTOM: Jewish General Hospital under construction, December, 1931. Part of an expanded hospital complex, this original structure is now called Pavilion B.

Medical Terms Used in This Book

Clinical Researcher Usually a specialist in an area of medicine, surgery, or psychiatry who then goes on to do basic cellular or molecular research, or ethical clinical research involving patients in clinical studies.

Division A part of a department, such as the Division of Cardiology in the Department of Medicine.

General Practitioner (GP) A physician who has usually trained for two years after completing medical school.

Grand Rounds Usually a lecture given by a specialist (whether in clinical or basic science) to the entire staff in a department. The subjects of such lectures are many, but the main purpose is to keep the medical community aware of the latest issues and developments in medicine.

Head Nurse A senior nurse who has had considerable experience in the area in which they work, and who organizes the functions of more junior nurses. To be a **Registered Nurse**, students need to pursue an Associate Degree in Nursing (two years) or a Bachelor of Science in Nursing (four years). This training covers a good deal of medical information as well as the specific aspects of nursing.

Intern or Rotating Intern In the past, "intern" was the term for medical graduates, with their newly achieved MD degrees, who were entering their first year of residency training at a hospital. During this year they would "rotate" between various specialties, and at different hospitals, to further their medical education. "Intern" has fallen out of use, and students today are simply referred to as entering their first year of residency training.

Hear no evil, see no evil, speak no evil!

Internist Internists are specialists in internal medicine. After medical school, young doctors must choose one of three routes: medicine, surgery, or psychiatry. After about five years of training, physicians in these areas are referred to as internists, general surgeons, or psychiatrists. Residents who choose to pursue further training in subspecialties *within* one of these three main routes are referred to by the title of their specialty (e.g., cardiologist, orthopedic surgeon, etc.).

Jewish General Hospital (**JGH**) Often referred to as the Jewish General or "the Jewish," the hospital was founded in 1934, from a bequest by Sir Mortimer Davis. Initially, this was to address a longstanding desire of Jewish Montrealers to have a hospital for their medical needs, along with the MGH and RVH. The hospital also assured appropriate training for Jewish doctors who had, at one time, had difficulty acquiring specialty medical training, shut out of the medical system in Quebec. The "Days of Shame" (discussed briefly in the "Physician-in-Chief" chapter) were a timely reminder of the dire need for such a hospital. The JGH, the MGH, and the RVH, along with all other Montreal hospitals, are now open to all patients regardless of race, religion, language, or ethnic background.

Medical School In Canada, students of medicine spend four years—first in the classroom, and then on hospital wards and clinics—to achieve their Doctor of Medicine degree (abbreviated MD, from the Latin *Medicinae Doctor*).

Montreal General Hospital (**MGH**) Often referred to simply as the General, the MGH was founded in 1819. It was Montreal's first English-language hos-

pital, and within a decade became the first teaching hospital in Canada. Indeed, the MGH was a major aspect in the founding of McGill University.

Orderly A person (commonly a man) who has not had formal medical education but who helps with patients, such as moving them to different areas of the hospital (e.g., to and from radiology or operating rooms).

Resident Residents are effectively physicians-in-training, or young doctors, who have recently received their university MD degree and who are now pursuing further training most frequently in the areas of medicine, surgery, or psychiatry. This initial specialty training usually takes three to five years. Physicians may then go on to train in subspecialties such as cardiology or gastroenterology, for another two or three years. Research training may follow.

Rounds Discussion between residents and/or attending staff about the health and care of individual patients at a particular point of their illness. These discussions can take place before the group visits a patient at the bedside, or afterward, depending on the situation or need.

The Royal Victoria Hospital (RVH) Often referred to as the "Royal Vic" or simply "the Vic," RVH was established in 1893 and became the other major hospital in the McGill Faculty of Medicine.

Senior Resident Residents in the last year of their training.

Specialist A physician who has had subspecialty training as described above (see “Resident”).

Staff Physicians, surgeons, and psychiatrists who have completed their training and who are hired by a hospital in their specialty are referred to as staff doctors. The old post of chief of staff is not really a job title in use in hospitals anymore.

Credits

Excerpts from "I've Always Loved You Best" by Erma Bombeck (pages 110, 115, and 119) are from *Forever, Erma* (Andrews McMeel, 1996). Bombeck republished and updated her popular essay several times.

Paintings by Evelyn Gold (pages 19, 45, 59, 70, 72, 108, 125) were completed around 2003, shown at the Mount Stephen Club in the exhibit *"I have often walked on that street before"* and are reprinted with other works in *What I Heard Where I Lived*, a limited-edition booklet of Yiddish maxims uttered by Chana Katz, Evelyn's mother.

All images courtesy of the author except the following:

4 Market: Public domain, from Wikipedia (Ozarow).

5 Memorial plaque: Mark Winograd (Mwinog2777) from Wikipedia (Opatow Ghetto).

5 Postcard: From Chapter 8 of *Memories of Ozarow* by Hillel Adler (1996), trans. William Fraiberg, image accessed via Yizkor Book Database at JewishGen.org.

6 Garment workers: Public Archives of Canada (A.C. Kells, PAC, PA116362). From *Times To Remember* by Knowlton Nash (Key Porter 1986).

8 *Jeunes garçons dans la rue* by Paul-Marc Auger, McCord Museum M2004.69.31.

9 Boulevard Saint-Laurent: 31 août 1944, Archives de la Ville de Montréal (VdM), VM94-Z2230-3.

10 Vintage ad from Wikipedia (Kodak Brownie).

14 Cugat covers: public domain, source unknown.

15 Baseball game at Delorimier Park, Montreal, QC, about 1933, McCord Museum MP-1985.31.187.

15 Robinson: Associated Press, digitalballparks.com.

15 Richard and Beliveau, 1958: Canadian Press.

20 Chip truck, 1947: VdM Archives, VM094-Z386-01.
21 Horse-drawn milk float, 1942: Alamy KXMGOD.
21 Elmhurst products: laiteriesduquebec.com.
22 Home ice delivery, 1920s: National Museum of American History, Sloane Collection.
22 Ice prices, City Ice Co., 1913. Emporium Collection.
22 Ice cutting, St. Lawrence River at Montreal, QC, about 1870, McCord Museum, MP-0000.1452.40.
25 Bancroft Snack Bar: histoireplateau.canal-blog.com, December 3, 2017. Source unknown.
25 *Peter and the Wolf* album cover: public domain.
26 *Lassie Come-Home* original cover: biblio.com.
27 Gold and Levy: Dario Ayala, *The Montreal Gazette*, February 13, 2017. Courtesy of Dario Ayala and Postmedia/*The Montreal Gazette*.
32 Avenue Mont-Royal parade, festival-commerce, 1941: SDAMR, BANQ, Fonds O. Allard, 74016307.
32 *Jour de la Victoire en Europe* by Conrad Poirier. Bibliothèque et Archives national de Quebec (BANQ), BANQ Vieux-Montréal, Fonds Conrad Poirier, P48,S1,P11845.
34 ILGWU label: Vintage North Blog, March 1, 2012.
34 ILGWU poster: Jewish Public Library (JPL) Archives.
34 Triangle Shirtwaist Fire: *The New York World*, March 26, 1911, Library of Congress, 98519347. From Wikipedia.
35 UJPO: Labour Zionist Center, c1952, JPL Archives.
36 Police locking door: *The Montreal Gazette*, Jan. 28, 1950. Image via Zev Moses, Third Solitude, April 20, 2012.
37 YMHA: VdM, CA M001 VM094-Y-1-17-D0127.
37 Sammy Jacobs, YMHA, c1939–1940: JPL Archives.
39 Rialto: VdM, CA M001 VM094-Y-1-17-D0118.
39 Regent: Library and Archives Canada. PA-119685.
40 Vieux-Lesage: Mon Musée Virtuel, Guy Thibault.
40 Iron lung: Hospital for Sick Children Archives.
42 Baron Byng exterior, 1970s: JPL Archives.
48 *Deux hommes, Port de Montréal*, by Paul-Marc Auger, 1938. McCord Museum, M2004.69.15.3.
49 Unloading Molasses: Museum of Science and Technology of Canada (MSTC), CN009867.
49 Bananas: MSTC, CN31279.
51 Steinberg's, 1920s: Jewish Publish Library Archives.
51 Trolley, 1944: Société de transport de Montréal (STM) Archives, via Tramways history webpage.
52 Brewery, 1995: CTV News archives.
52 Bottles: Ecomusée du Fier Monde, Molson collection.
54 Encyclopedia ads: Source unknown.
55 2110 Bedford Road: Still from Google Streetview.
57 2022 Sternthal Building: Derek Webster, March.
58 1952 Pontiac: www.oldcarandtruck pictures.com.
62 Roddick Gates postcard: BANQ.
64 James Bldg: David Boardman, manchesterhistory.net.
64 *Professor Sir Arnold Burgen* by June Mendoza: Darwin College, University of Cambridge.
66 Strathcona Building: McGill University Archives.

71 L'Echourie: Still from *Artist in Montreal* (NFB, 1954).
71 Plasticiens poster by Arthur Gladu et Gérald Brunet, 1955: Musée National des Beaux Arts de Québec (MNBAQ).
76 Duplessis laying stone, 2 May 1953: Art & Heritage Centre of the MUHC, Mann Fonds, 2017-0001.04.2.11.
77 Drawing: Art & Heritage Centre of the MUHC, Berkovitz Fonds.
78 Nurses: Archives of the Alumnae Association of the Montreal General Hospital School of Nursing.
81 Orange Julep: M. Macot, VdM, VM94-A0162-018.
82 *OR no. 10*, painting by Albert Cloutier: collection of Dr. David Mulder, courtesy of Medical Multimedia Department of the MUHC. Photograph by Michael Cichon.
83 Dr. H. Rocke Robertson: Art & Heritage Centre of the MUHC, Berkovitz Fonds, 2014-0014.04.2167.
85 View of MGH: Art & Heritage Centre of the MUHC, Berkovitz Fonds, 2014-0014.04.473.2.
88 Cardiac Monitoring Unit, c. 1970. Art & Heritage Centre of the MUHC, Berkovitz Fonds, 2104-0014.04.669.2.
90 MGH Residents and staff: courtesy of Dr. Phil Gold.
90 Jane Fonda, *Life* magazine, April 23, 1971: Blog of thefilmexperience.net, December 18, 2021.
92 Dr. Ian Henderson: Art & Heritage Centre of the MUHC, Berkovitz Fonds, 2014-0014.04.569.1.
92 Cobalt-60: The Canadian Illustrated Library, J.J. Brown, *The Inventors* (1967). Source unknown.
94 Dr. Carl Goresky, 1976: Art & Heritage Centre of the MUHC, Berkovitz Fonds, 2014-0014.04.816.
96 Images of CEA: courtesy of Dr. Phil Gold.
98 Architectural drawing of the MGH Research Institute: Art & Heritage Centre of the MUHC, Berkovitz Fonds.
100 *Le pavillon "L'Homme interroge l'Univers" et le pavillon des États-Unis à l'Expo 67* by Gabor Szilasi, 1967. BANQ Vieux-Montréal, E6,S7,SS1,P671461.
101 Midtown Skyline at Night, New York, 1968: Alamy.
103 Vintage ad, 1931: Phil Beard, Flickr.
103 Vintage pack: Canada 1950s, 20 pieces in Sliding Box, from Zigsam, the Austrian Cigarette Collection.
103 William Talman: Still from anti-smoking PSA, American Cancer Society, 1968. YouTube.
105 Sir Peter Medawar: NPG, London.
105 Sir Arnold Burgen, 1976: IMS Vintage.
105 Gold and Shuster: Meropi Vourvakis, MGH.
130 Goodman Cancer Institute: Tom Arban and Marc Cramer for Provencher Roy architects, provencherroy.ca.
133 Dr. Douglas Cameron, 1967: Art & Heritage Centre of the MUHC, Berkovitz Fonds, 2014-0014.04.851.
134 MGH (historical drawing): MGH 200.com.
134 MGH today: Mike Haimes, MGH Foundation.
135 Oswald Wellisch Chief Carpenter: MGH200.com.
138 Emil Skamene: Art & Heritage Centre of the MUHC, Berkovitz Fonds 2014-0014.04.976.
138 Joe Shuster, MUHC Archive, 2014-0014.04.1055.2.
141 The Cruesses: MUHC Archives, 2015-0002.04.171.
148 Anthony Jenkins, *The Globe and Mail*, September 8, 1984. Personal collection of Dr. Phil Gold. Courtesy of Anthony Jenkins and *The Globe and Mail*.
151 Dr. Phil Gold and students: Still from video for Canadian Medical Hall of Fame induction, 2010.

152 Sir William Osler, 1905: Wellcome Library, 13320i.

165 *Roddick Gates, McGill* by Terry Tomalty: courtesy of Phil and Evelyn Gold.

179 Motel Raphael, 1968: Photo by W. Schermer.

180 *Hôpital Sainte-Justine* by Conrad Poirier, June 6, 1944. BAnQ, BAnQ Vieux-Montreal, Fonds Conrad Poirier, P48, S1,P10647.

180 Jewish General Hospital, Montreal, under construction, Dec. 18, 1931. JGH Archives.